The Collector's Encyclopedia of
SALT & PEPPER
SHAKERS

Figural and Novelty
SECOND SERIES

BY
MELVA R. DAVERN

Edited by
Mary Schinhofen

COLLECTOR BOOKS
Division of Schroeder Publishing Co. Inc.

SEARCHING FOR A PUBLISHER?

We are always looking for knowlegeable people considered to be experts within their fields. If you feel that there is a real need for a book on your collectible subject and have a large comprehensive collection, contact Collector Books.

Additional copies of this book may be ordered from:

Collector Books
P.O. Box 3009
Paducah, Ky. 42002-3009

OR

Melva R. Davern
Box 81914
Pittsburgh, Pa. 15217

@$24.95 Add $2.00 for postage and handling.

Copyright: Melva R. Davern, 1990
Updated Values, 1995

DEDICATION

I dedicate this book, in memory, to my DAD. To the members of our family, he was our backbone. He taught us love and respect towards all people. He taught us to stand up for ourselves and always do the best we could.

My Dad worked forty hard years in a steel mill to make a good home for five children and a loving wife. We were not rich, but we never wanted for anything.

One never realizes just how much we love a parent until that day comes, and they are gone. I'm thankful that my Dad knew how much he was loved while he was still here. I guess this is my final way of saying "Thank you Dad."

ACKNOWLEDGMENTS

My thanks to all the collectors out there who were so pleased with Book One that it prompted Book Two! Bill Schroeder has again given me the opportunity to share my knowledge with the thousands of collectors around the world. I thank him.

My family tolerates a lot while I am preparing these books. There is often not a place to eat dinner, with the table covered with shakers or strewn with paper work! The shifting of boxes from one place to another has become the family pastime! So, to my loving husband of twenty-five years, George; my daughter Laura Burdette, (I gained a wonderful son-in-law, Scott, since Book One); and to my three sons, George Jr., Jack and Jason, thank you.

Although I lost my Dad in October of 1987, his lifelong encouragement will last me the rest of my life. I have again shared my childhood adventures with you throughout this book, so I can't forget to thank my wonderful mother, Barbara Beynon, who is still always there. My brothers and sisters still make life fun and are always there for me for any reason. Joanne Thiry, Jack and Bill Beynon, and Dolores Himelright, make up the best family one could ever ask for.

People laughed at "ALL" I thanked in Book One, and asked jokingly, "Did you forget anyone?" Well I did forget a very important person. Most people joke about their mother-in-law; however, I have one of the greatest little Irish mothers-in-law in the world. Nora Davern has babysat, sent me home-made pies, and evokes more encouragement than any ten people I know. I thank her for twenty-five years of love.

The trip to Kentucky for photographing this time merits a book of its own! But I will spare you the details. My collector friend, Carol Jessen, of Pittsburgh, made the trip with me this time. We did get there, we even stopped to visit friends along the way. Carol was a great help, even though she poured a gallon of iced tea all over me in the car! Her knowledge in areas of the book I was unsure of was quite helpful. There are not too many friends one can ask to come on a week long trip to pack and unpack fifty boxes as well as load and unload them from the car! I must thank her husband Jack also for allowing her to go, even though he did pay me to take her! Thanks Carol, it's only the real friends we can kid this way! Love ya.

Tom Clouser of Curtis & Mays Studio in Paducah was eagerly awaiting our arrival!! He did the great photography for Book One. His good humor and patience made three long days of shifting 1,500 sets of shakers around more of a pleasure than a task. Thanks again, Tom.

Steve Quertermous from Schroeder Publishing is the chief overseer of all the work on the book. He puts up with me calling all year long, yet he still showed up! His expertise in arranging the shakers and designing the cover, along with many hours of editing, is what makes authors, like myself, proud to have our name on a Collector Book. Many thanks, Steve.

Teri Hatch of Schroeder's was also there to assist Steve. She was a super help as well. I'm sure she knows more about salt and pepper shakers now than many collectors!

The list of people to thank is long so I will just say to all of you: without all your help and support, this book could not have been written. The period of time, over which this book was written, was often a sad and trying time for me and my family. Nevertheless, you all stayed close and offered support and encouragement, and never let me down. In whatever way you helped, I love and thank ALL of you. It is not an easy task to write a book and it is NEVER done alone.

Special thanks, first, to Trish Claar who spent endless hours in the Patent Office and libraries searching out much of the information used throughout this book.

Second, I must mention Theresa "TEE" Knox. She sends me more surprise packages of shakers as well as cartoon glasses (my other hobby!), than one could imagine. She has been a great friend and lends much support, since long before Book One was published.

Now on to the random list of my "Great Support System": Sylvia Tompkins, Marcia and Gene Smith, Larry Carey, Rich O'Donnell, Nigel Dalley, Floyd and Betty Carson, Bill and Joyce Fisher, Betsy Zalewski, Jim and Irene Thornburg, Jeannie Fouts, Linda McPherson, Dot Gammon, John Sirbaugh, Kay and Patsy Ramsey and Muriel O'Conner. All are members of the salt and pepper club, and I thank them for their contributions to this book.

To just a few close friends, whose main contribution was to call "every day" to ask: "Is the book done yet?" I finished it just to get you off my back! They are: Rose and Jack Hertzer, Jean and Gene Burik, Carol and Buzzy Boross, and Anna and Donna "Purple Passion" Gray.

People who loaned me shakers are mentioned throughout the book. To ALL of you, "thank you." This is YOUR book.

Last, but far from least is my "Buddy" and dearest friend, Mary Schinhofen. She has again transformed most of this book into English! She spent many, many hours re-typing the pages herein. I am most thankful she can "spell," because I cannot! She can correct and edit so much, yet she always seems to be able to leave my strange sense of humor intact! For all of this Mary, as well as our many wonderful years of friendship, I truly "thank you."

It has been five years since the first book was released. It seems like it took an eternity to finish this one. I hope when you see the contents, you will feel the long wait was worthwhile.......

THE NOVELTY SALT AND PEPPER SHAKER CLUB

In July of 1991 the Novelty Salt and Pepper Collectors Club passed the 1200 mark in members. With the help and dedication of many members, this goal was reached. The club has held annual conventions in Pittsburgh, Battle Creek, Cleveland, Memphis and Chicago and plan 1992 for Vermont and 1993 for Florida.

Many members have had articles written about them in local papers, magazines, antique and collectibles publications and several major newspapers. The club has been contacted by *United Press International* and *Associated Press* for information about shakers and collectors for articles about our hobby. Several members have done television interviews about their collection. All of this has helped to build our club faster than any other collectors club we have been involved with.

The officers of our club have always been very dedicated. We have all worked well together to give our membership the best newsletter in the collectibles arena. The new research and superb articles make this publication an asset to all collectors. The involvement of the membership in supplying articles and information about their own collection has helped to give collectors the best available information about salt and pepper shakers and their history. A collection is always more interesting when you know all you can about the sets you have.

We have been so very lucky to have two excellent newsletter editors. Soon we will change for the third time to a new editor. Each time the search for the right person has been a success. Our newsletter has always been the backbone of our club. Thanks to all of you who have dedicated your time to keeping it the very best we could ask for.

My term of office as President of the Novelty Salt and Pepper Club ended this July with the election of new officers. After four years in office, I chose not to run again. I feel new blood and new ideas will help the club grow more each year. I will always be a dedicated member of this club. I am very grateful to all the people who help make it the best. It has been a pleasure to fill the office of President since its first election in 1987. I have worked with the best officers and newsletter editors one could ask for. I know we will all work together in the future years to keep our club together and continue to provide our members with the best, most informative and interesting newsletter possible.

If you wish to join the club and receive our quarterly newsletter, Please write to:

Irene Thornburg, Membership Coordinator
581 Joy Rd.
Battle Creek, Michigan 49017

Dues at this time are $20.00 per year, $25.00 for overseas. Please enclose a self-addressed, stamped envelope if you just seek information when writing.

Other Salt and Pepper Clubs

British Novelty Salt and Pepper Collectors Club
c/o Ray Dodd
'Cole Hill; Clayton Road
Mold, CLWYD, CH7 ISX
England

New Zealand Salt and Pepper Club
c/o Jean Neilson
35 Orepuki/Riverton Rd
Riverton
Southland N.Z.

Please enclose S.A.S.E. for all clubs

"THE FUTURE OF COLLECTING SHAKERS RESTS IN OUR HANDS"

I have always felt that the best part of "collecting," is the people you meet along the way. The annual conventions we have each year have opened up an entirely new avenue to pursue. Prior to the conventions, many of us kept in touch for years by mail or phone, always considering each other friends, yet rarely having the opportunity to actually meet. Now, we have collectors from all over the world and from all the states gathering together to meet each other. Those names and voices on the phone are becoming real people. In turn, those people are becoming great friends. We are getting to know other collectors from our own states, and often the same towns. One of our plans for the future is to have state or area chapters of the club. This will help build our annual conventions, because collectors can get together in carpools or just arrange to travel together.

The past few years have brought about another trend. Many collectors plan their vacation routes to include stops at other collector's homes to see their collections. This must always be prearranged; however, there are many people who welcome other collectors to come and view their collections.

The best method to further your knowledge of what is still out there for you to find for your own collections, is to get out and see what other people have. I have never yet seen another collection that did not include at least one set I had never seen before. I find any assortment of shakers fascinating to look at, be it ten or ten thousand.

I have been told that the set-up of my book drives people crazy! Because they like the system, they spend days rearranging their own collections! Considering that people most often collect in specialized areas, this is an easy way for them to locate their speciality. This also holds true with a large collection. It is much easier to look at, if all the shakers are categorized. Especially if you have a visiting collector, whose interest is in a specific area, you will know right where those shakers are. Happy Re-Arranging!!

Did you ever read about someone else's collection, of anything, in a magazine or newspaper? Or see a collector on television telling the world about his favorite thing to collect? Well, keep in mind that people in the television and publishing businesses are always looking for ideas or collectors to feature. Believe me, it is much easier for you to find them, than it is for them to find you! Write to everyone about your collection. It is a super way to let people know, not only about your hobby, but also about our club. It is a good idea to "never" give your address with any published article. However, you can list the current club address (or MY address to order this book!!). I always have collectors sending me articles from their hometown newspapers, and I love to receive them and do keep them all.

When you cross paths with people who laugh when you tell them what you collect, don't back off, EDUCATE THEM! Be proud of your collection. By all means involve your entire family. I can assure you that if they really look at what you collect and more than that, UNDERSTAND it, you can be sure that if they buy you shakers in their travels, it will be something fitting! Make sure your family knows what to do with your collection, once you are gone. Keeping good records will help, as well as a periodic update of values. This may sound morbid to some, but it is a fact of life, we will all leave this world one of these days! I want to know my family AND my collection is taken care of!

Many new shakers are being issued each year. Keep any advertisements or catalogs about shakers. Keep all your newsletters in a file with the record about your collection. If your collection is passed on to another family member, or sold, make sure this material goes with it. If we work together to accumulate all the information we can on the old sets as well as the sets in the future, collectors for years to come will benefit from our efforts to preserve the history of salt and pepper shakers.

I look forward to having "OUR" place in a museum someday. By then, we should have a great supply of information. My first book came out in 1985 but *this book* is entirely different in content. Helene Guarnaccia has two books on the market and a book written by Gideon Bosker was published in 1986. Many other books have included full pages of shakers; before we only saw a few. Take heed collectors. We even merit a "Salt and Pepper Shakers" listing in some of the general price guides! This is progress!

My hope is to have the 1997 annual convention back here in Pittsburgh, where the "New" club began. My wish is to see at least 1,000 collectors in attendance! My feelings are it will happen! Happy Collecting!

BOOKS HELPFUL TO COLLECTORS

Lehner's Encyclopedia of U.S. Marks
Lois Lehner

The Collector's Enclyclopedia of Shakers, 1985
Melva R. Davern

Salt and Pepper Shakers 1 & 2
Helene Guarnaccia

(Books above can be ordered from Collector Books)

Great Shakes, 1986
Gideon Bosker
Abeville Press, 505 Park Ave. New York, New York, 10022

Blue Ridge Dinnerware
Bill and Betty Newbound

Purinton Pottery
Pat Dole,
P.O. Box 4782, Birmingham, Alabama 35206

Rosemeade Pottery
Irene Harms
2316 West 18th St., Sioux Falls, South Dakota, 57104

CLUBS

Novelty Salt and Pepper Shakers Club
Irene Thornburg
581 Joy Road, Battle Creek, Michigan 49017

Cat Collectors
31311 Blair Drive, Warren, Michigan 48092

TABLE OF CONTENTS

AMERICA BY PARKCRAFT

When I had the photography done for this book in October, 1987, I was thrilled because I had managed to borrow the entire series of State Shakers to share with you in this book. Nigel Dalley, my collector friend from England, had just bought the set here in the United States and was kind enough to leave them with me until I had them photographed. Thanks, Nigel!

Although the state series is very collectible, we all seem to keep asking what goes with which and vice versa. I felt that it was important to try to show the entire series as well as to supply the original list for the 48 states and the list for the 50-state series. Although I hope to answer many of the questions, I must say at the outset that not all of you will have exactly the same pieces that I have pictured; many sets are from a combination of both series. I do know that the orange used with California is not the correct one; I used it, however, to let you know that another type of orange does indeed go with this state.

As you all well know, it is difficult to obtain information about many of the sets we collect. I had many "bits and pieces" of information about Parkcraft to share with you until I attended the Salt-and-Pepper Convention of 1988. For those of you who know me well, the thought of rendering ME speechless smacks of improbability. I must, however, credit Larry Carey with a first! For several months prior to the convention, Larry had talked about a surprise guest speaker that he was attempting to locate. We all of course just humored Larry as we normally do when he breaks out with one of his enthusiastic whims!! Well, I must admit that I was left speechless because I had to eat my words. Larry came through magnificently and I know it will be a long time before anyone can upstage the 1988 convention.

The guests were Bob and Marianne Ahrold – the folks who founded the Parkcraft Company back in 1949. The thrill of having them present swept the room which was full of collectors from all over the United States as well as from England and Canada. They and their family have made a contribution to our world of collecting that will forever be remembered. The Parkcraft line of salt and pepper shakers continue to be one of the most sought after in the history of this collectible. At this point, it is difficult to determine who was more thrilled – the collectors or the Ahrolds who were overwhelmed by their reception. Personally speaking, I can think of little that could have meant more to me. Those of you who do research can understand the importance of being able to talk to real live people about a company that had been their "baby." Books are usually our only resource...so this event was really super, super special.

I will tell you more about Parkcraft as we go along, but first allow me to discuss this page of shakers before going on. I have the shakers set up in alphabetical order. This page begins with Alaska with its igloo through to Kansas and wheat. Included on the first shelf are the flags of the United States, also made by Parkcraft. Many people include this set with their states collection and I find it to be quite appropriate to fly our flag over these beautiful shakers!

Since the Ahrolds are from Burlington, Iowa, it is no surprise that the first state set they designed was Iowa and its corn companion. You will notice on the lists at the end of this section that the list with the fifty states has many different objects listed as companions for the states when compared to the first list. This was to ensure that no companion object was repeated when the second series was issued. Alaska and Hawaii, the last two states to join our Union, are pictured on this first page.

Row 1:   Set Two: Flags – $45.00-$50.00
All 50 State Sets – $22.00-$25.00 each set

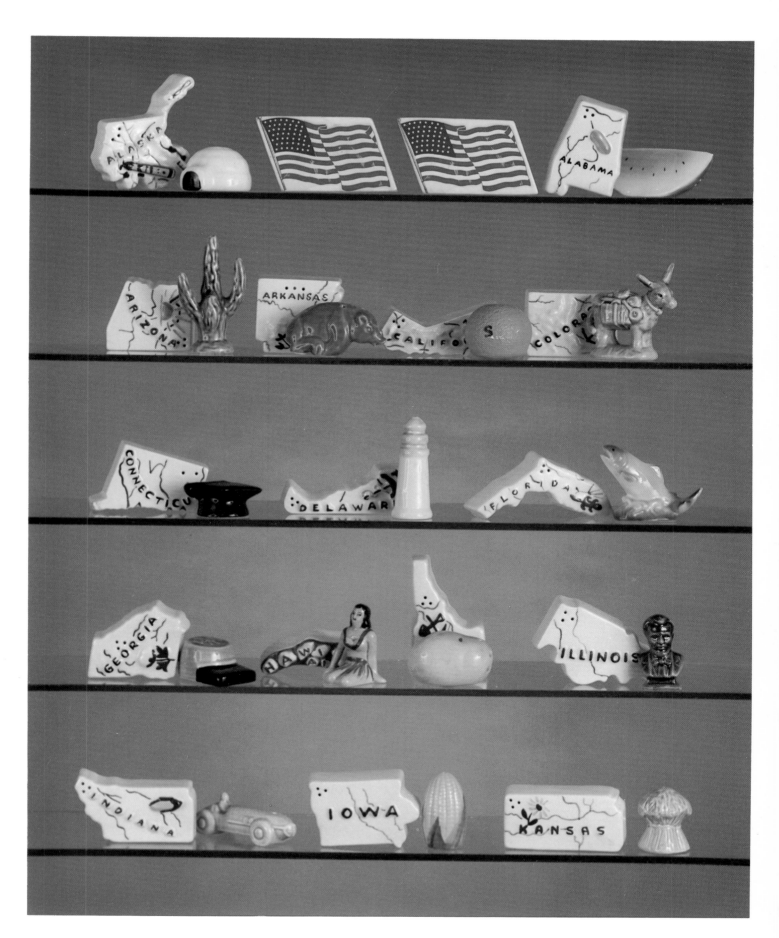

This page begins with Kentucky and a jug and ends with North Carolina and a pack of cigarettes, with many wonderful sets in between. One may wonder how these sets were determined and I can assure you that they were not just picked randomly. Bob Ahrold cared enough to research the product to go with each state; he took the time to contact the governors of all the states, requesting their ideas and preferences on the product which would best represent their state. This family took a great deal of pride in Parkcraft and the items they produced prove it.

It would be interesting to speculate just how many of these symbols have become obsolete with the changing times. Coal and some farm products, for example, are no longer as important as they once were. I think that I may speak for other collectors as well as myself....It's not too late to create a third series of states, Bob!!! We need an update!

Most of the series sets designed by Parkcraft were manufactured by the Taneycomo Ceramic Factory of Hollister, Mo. These sets include: the forty-eight and fifty states series; the famous cities series consisting of 18 sets which include famous cities from around the world as well as in the United States; the months of the year; twelve sets comprised of a cylindrical shaker with the name of the month on it and an object commonly related to that month, i.e., February and a heart, June and a wedding cake, and October and a pumpkin. A "famous people" series was made up of seven sets which has collectors scurrying to find them all. While you are writing to Bob about the "new" state series, it wouldn't hurt to remind him about all the famous people we have had since the last "famous people" series was issued! Maybe we can convince him we need several new updates.

In the 1960's Parkcraft also issued a "Days of the Week" series: Monday was washday, Tuesday was ironing day, Wednesday was sewing day. Thursday was visiting day, Friday was cleaning day, Saturday was baking day and of course, Sunday was church day. The original price of $8.50 for the entire series could not purchase even one set today! A series of twelve miniature nursery rhyme sets were also designed by Parkcraft; both of these series were manufactured in Japan for the company.

$22.00-$25.00 per set

LIST OF PARKCRAFT STATE SETS

First Set: 48 States c. 1957

Alabama	Cotton
Arizona	Cactus
Arkansas	Razorback
California	Bathing Beauty
Colorado	Pack Mule
Connecticut	Graduation Cap
Delaware	Lighthouse
Florida	Bathing Beauty
Georgia	Confederate Cap
Idaho	Potato
Illinois	Corn
Indiana	Racer
Iowa	Corn
Kansas	Wheat
Kentucky	Jug
Louisiana	Cotton
Maine	Lighthouse
Maryland	Oyster
Massachusetts	Bean Pot
Michigan	Car
Minnesota	Canoe
Mississippi	Cotton
Missouri	Mule
Montana	Six Shooter
Nebraska	Corn
Nevada	Ace of Spades
New Hampshire	Snowman
New Jersey	Miss America
New Mexico	Pueblo
New York	Statue of Liberty
North Carolina	Cigarettes
North Dakota	Wheat
Ohio	Tire
Oklahoma	Oil Well
Oregon	Duck
Pennsylvania	Coal
Rhode Island	Rooster
South Carolina	Lighthouse
South Dakota	Pheasant
Tennessee	Cotton
Texas	Oil Well
Utah	Covered Wagon
Vermont	Maple Syrup Bucket
Virginia	Ham
Washington	Apple
West Virginia	Coal
Wisconsin	Cheese
Wyoming	Bronco

This final page begins with North Dakota and an oil well and ends the entire series with Wyoming and a bronco. I hope the illustrations of the entire set will help many of you in your search to complete your series.

At the convention, we lovingly dubbed Bob "Mr. Parkcraft" since he had handled the designing and manufacturing end of the business. Marianne in turn was named "Mrs. Heather House," since this was the mail order firm which handled the distribution of the Parkcraft products and which was her responsibility. In talking to this wonderful couple at length, one could sense the pride in their firm emanating from each of them. Their children became a part of the business as well, working together with the employees to do anything which needed to be done, including packing orders. Heather House is still in business as a mail order house, selling souvenir and gift items but fewer shakers than before...but we can change that!

Many of you, I am sure, remember the Heather House catalogs of the 1950's and 1960's. Many of the shakers in our collections today were purchased from these catalogs. Most of the sets sold for $1.00 with all types of bonuses for club members. Throughout this catalog were articles lovingly written about the new sets being introduced, answers to questions sent in by collectors, and offering information in general. This column, which created much enthusiasm among the collectors, was by Mari Jill. Many of you may recognize the name as well as remembering how much you enjoyed reading her articles. Several of the S & P club members, including me, had tried to locate Mari Jill without success. In July of 1988, however, all of this changed. We at last found Mari Jill; she is, in fact, Marianne Ahrold, our "Mrs. Heather House"! She did not merely sell to customers; she and her family genuinely cared about the people the company dealt with and had a close relationship with so many of them. I told Marianne that people would remember her...to prove it, I have included her address at Heather House at the end of this section. Drop the Ahrolds a note just to let them know you appreciate their contribution to your collecting memories. If you don't remember them first hand, just write and let them know how much you love the sets that they so proudly produced.

I, of course, "owed" Larry Carey for his great accomplishment and the fifth of liquid refreshment I bestowed upon him was simply a small token of our appreciation. Another great big thank you to Larry from all of us for the wonderful surprise. And, as president of the Novelty Salt and Pepper Shaker Collector's Club, may I again say thanks to both Bob and Marianne Ahrold for honoring us with their presence at the 1988 convention.

$22.00-$25.00 per set

Second Set: 50 States c. 1968

State	Item	State	Item
Alaska	Igloo	Montana	Six Shooter
Alabama	Watermelon	Nebraska	Cowboy Boots
Arizona	Cactus	Nevada	Ace of Spades
Arkansas	Razorback	New Hampshire	Snowman
California	Orange	New Jersey	Miss America
Colorado	Pack Mule	New Mexico	Pueblo
Connecticut	Graduation Cap	New York	Statue of Liberty
Delaware	Lighthouse	North Carolina	Cigarettes
Florida	Fish	North Dakota	Oil Well
Georgia	Confederate Cap	Ohio	Tire
Hawaii	Native Girl	Oklahoma	Indian
Idaho	Potato	Oregon	Duck
Illinois	Lincoln	Pennsylvania	Liberty Bell
Indiana	Racer	Rhode Island	Rooster
Iowa	Corn	South Carolina	Cotton
Kansas	Wheat	South Dakota	Pheasant
Kentucky	Jug	Tennessee	Horse Head
Louisiana	Sugar Sack	Texas	Cowboy Hat
Maine	Pine Tree	Utah	Covered Wagon
Maryland	Oyster	Vermont	Maple Syrup Bucket
Massachusetts	Bean Pot	Virginia	Ham
Michigan	Car	Washington	Apple
Minnesota	Canoe	West Virginia	Coal
Mississippi	Steamboat	Wisconsin	Cheese
Missouri	Mule	Wyoming	Bronco

BLUE RIDGE AND PURINTON

Southern Potteries of Erwin, Tennessee, manufactured the beautiful "Blue Ridge Dinnerware" shakers, featured on the first two shelves of this section. The first and last sets in Row One are called "Bud Top." The remaining sets in this row are "Blossom Top." All of the shakers in Row Two are tall "China Sets." All of the shakers are beautifully hand painted. The china sets in Row Two were decorated by using different mixtures of patterns from the dinnerware so that the shakers could be used with a number of different dinnerware settings. The prices on "Blue Ridge" items have been rapidly on the rise. I have seen the prices on these shakers more than double in just a couple of years. The dinnerware is outstanding, and the other items made have a uniqueness about them that has been lost in more recent years. Automation has eliminated that charming, hand painted elegance once used by many of the old china and pottery companies.

Blue Ridge was produced from late 1930 until 1956. There are several excellent books written concerning this company. (see reference list.)

The last two rows of shakers were made by Purinton Pottery. They also are wonderfully hand-painted. There are so many designs to be found as well as quite a few one-of-a-kind pieces. Pat Dole, editor of the "New Glaze," wrote a book outlining the history of Purinton Pottery. She features many different patterns which is a great help in trying to identify unusual Purinton items. (see reference list.)

Puriton Pottery began operations in Wellsville, Ohio, in 1936. It moved to Shippenville, Pennsylvania in 1941, and closed its doors in 1959.

There are just a few of the designs featured in the shakers I have. In Row Three, the first set is the "Palm Tree" pattern. The third set in this row is called "Open Apple." Both sets are "pour and shake" style shakers. The center set is a range set; I do not know the name of the floral pattern it bears. In the fourth row the first and last shakers are jug style. The patterns are "Apple" on the first set, and "Normandy Plaid" on the last set. The plaid comes in several colors. The second set in Row Four has the fruit pattern. I do not know the name of the pattern of the third set, nor do I know the styles of the center two sets.

Purinton is one of the American companies to keep your eye on. It is becoming increasingly difficult to find many of these shakers. Sets included in this section are courtesy of Carol Jessen.

Row 1:	All sets: $45.00-$55.00 per set			
Row 2:	All sets: $45.00-$55.00 per set			
Row 3:	(1) $55.00-$60.00	(2) $45.00-$50.00	(3) $45.00-$50.00	
Row 4:	(1) $15.00-$20.00	(2) $25.00-$30.00	(3) $30.00-$35.00	(4) $15.00-$20.00

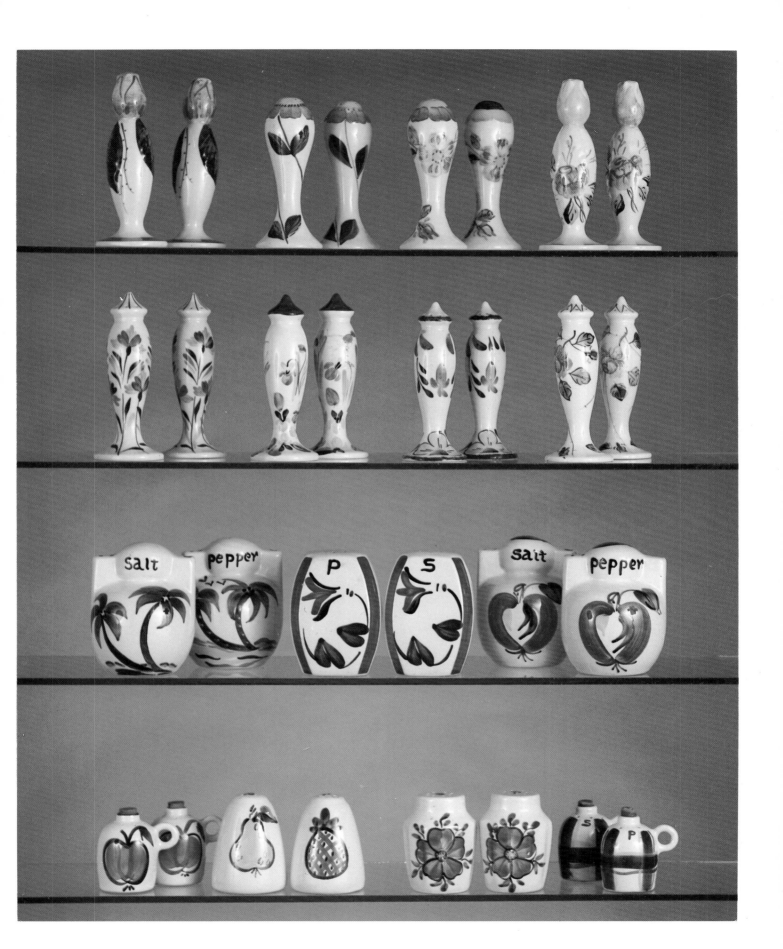

CERAMIC ARTS STUDIO: HARRINGTON CREATIONS

This wonderful assortment of shakers was designed by Betty Harrington and manufactured by the Ceramic Arts Studio of Madison, Wisconsin. The detail of Harrington's work creates a charm in her figurines instantly recognizable to the collector, even without an identifiying mark. If you study the "feel" of the glaze, the types of clay used, and the style of the painting (including the rosy cheeks she so often specified), you will be able to spot more and more of these quaility sets to add to your collection.

This Ceramic Arts Studio was in operation from 1941 until 1955. The earlier pre-automation years are credited with having produced the finer work: when automated production was introduced, much of the "personal touch" was lost. All of the products made by this company, however, are still very collectible and the prices reflect their desirability.

Thanks to the generosity of Betty Carson, I have two pages of wonderful shakers to share with you. The first and third sets in Row One are "Oak Sprite" sitting on a leaf. Both sets are adorable. In the center of the row is a deer and fawn, painted in an olive green and delightfully stylized.

In Row Two, we have "Wee Eskimos," "Wee Chinese" and "Wee Indians"--all with the characteristic rosy cheeks. In Row Three are boy and girl pigs cleverly dressed. The large Dutch people are next. The last set in this row is very ingenious, as you can see; the trunks of the elephants are formed into the letters "S" and "P"! The Spaniels in Row Four are beautifully rendered as is "Suzette," the poodle on the pillow. The last set on this page is entitled "Ram" and "Ewe," a delightfully imaginative interpretation.

Row 1: (1) $50.00-$60.00	(2) $65.00-$75.00	(3) $50.00-$60.00
Row 2: (1) $30.00-$35.00	(2) $22.00-$25.00	(3) $30.00-$35.00
Row 3: (1) $35.00-$40.00	(2) $30.00-$45.00	(3) $35.00-$40.00
Row 4: (1) $55.00-$60.00	(2) $55.00-$60.00	(3) $55.00-$60.00

CERAMIC ARTS STUDIO (continued)

The set on the top row of this page is also featured on the cover of this book. It is one of the most beautiful shaker sets I have ever seen. Not only is the coloring totally realistic, but the way the shakers are formed also contributes to the effect of miniature real-life leopards. It is in addition, a bit larger than the other shakers and therefore, a bit more imposing.

In the center of Row Two is a set of brown bears; a mother and her cub. The Ceramic Arts Studio did a series of mother-and-baby sets which proved to be very popular. This series is usually signed with the Ceramic Arts Studio logo.

In the center of Row Three is a frog and toadstool. This set is extremely colorful and very well done. All the sets in this row would make a nice addition to a water-related collection as well as to any general collection.

The first set in Row Four is entitled "Chip" and "Chirp" (printed on the bottom of each shaker.) The little mouse resting inside the wedge of cheese is another favorite among collectors. Although there are many versions of the mouse-and-cheese sets, this is the only set signed by Ceramic Arts Studio.

The remaining sets on this page are all unique in some way and they are all very collectible. Just as with any quality set, the prices continue to rise, so don't pass any up! If space is problem, this is a good area for a specialized collection. The number of sets are limited, they are all American-made, worth collecting, and I assure you that the demand for these sets will soon far outweigh the supply.

Also, a word of advice...If you find figurines or other pieces made by the Ceramic Arts Studio, don't pass them up. These pieces are also hard to find and will provide good "trading material" for shakers.

Row 1: All $125.00-150.00
Row 2: (1) $40.00-$45.00   (2) $45.00-$55.00   (3) $35.00-$40.00
Row 3: (1) $45.00-$50.00   (2) $35.00-$40.00   (3) $35.00-$40.00
Row 4: (1) $60.00-$65.00   (2) $25.00-$28.00   (3) $40.00-$45.00

ROSEMEADE AND FRANKOMA

While photographing for Book One, I came across a set of Rosemeade shakers. Since it was too late to do any research on them, I promised my readers a page devoted to Rosemeade in this book. I made a serious error in my discussion of these shakers, however, in stating that they all have a shiny black glaze. To my great surprise (and chagrin), I have since learned that Rosemeade sets come in many color variations...as you can see in the photograph.

The sets were made from 1940 to 1961 by the Wahpeton Pottery Company located in Wahpeton, North Dakota. Rosemeade is the trade name for the company. Many pieces are unmarked; if you study the texture of the fired North Dakota clay, however, you will soon learn to recognize it even without markings. The unglazed bottoms of the pieces seem to have a special "sparkle" about them. Study the colors and texture of Rosemeade the next time that you are at a pottery show and you will see what I mean. If you are interested in learning more about this company, a book entitled "Beautiful Rosemeade" was released in 1986 and is listed in the reference section. In addition to relating the history of the Wahpeton Pottery Company, it contains loads of illustrations.

Yes, I know! The brown bears in the middle of Row One are not a set; they should be paired the same as the black bears on the end. I hope this may help others with mismatched sets feel better! In addition, the first set of shakers in Row Two are not bowling pins-they are pelicans! (I must apologize for not turning some of these sets sideways so that you could see them better-one never knows what the photographs will reveal until very late in the game.) The center set in Row Three are black chickens and from left to right in Row Four are sets of quail, black swans and small birds.

The Rosemeade sets are very popular with collectors and the prices are usually hefty! My thanks to Betty Carson, good friend to so many of us, for the generous loan of her Rosemeade sets-as well as other sets from her collection.

In order for you to get an idea of what to look for when searching for American-made shakers, I have included a sampling of Frankoma sets. Frankoma, a family-owned company which is still in business, is located in Sapulpa, Oklahoma. The company opened in 1936 and has been twice rebuilt as a result of two devastating fires which leveled it. In order to be able to recognize Frankoma pottery, one must again study both the clay and the glazes used by this company. Many other sets of shakers were made by Frankoma in addition to the sets pictured here, and several books which focus upon Frankoma pottery have been published.

Both Rosemeade and Frankoma have full lines of pottery items. Avid collectors of American-made items continually search for these and other examples of American pottery-a fine choice as well for the shaker collector.

Row 1:	(1) $45.00-$65.00	(2) $35.00-$40.00	(3) $35.00-$40.00
Row 2:	(1) $50.00-$60.00	(2) $40.00-$50.00	(3) $30.00-$35.00
Row 3	(1) $40.00-$50.00	(2) $75.00-$85.00	(3) $30.00-$40.00
Row 4	(1) $35.00-$40.00	(2) $40.00-$50.00	(3) $30.00-$35.00
Row 5	All Sets: $15.00-$18.00		

SHAWNEE POTTERY

All of the sets on the page were made by the Shawnee Pottery Company, located in Zanesville, Ohio. The company began production in 1937 and made many wonderful items before it closed its doors in 1961. All Shawnee Pottery is collectible today. Two of the most popular areas of collecting are cookie jars and of course, salt and pepper shakers. The prices continue to rise on the shaker sets; the gold trimmed sets merit even a higher price.

My thanks to Carol Jessen for the loan of most of the Shawnee for this section.

In the top row, we have the large Dutch couple, the large Boy Pigs, (both of these sets are five inches tall) and the Dutch children. The second row consists of the five inch Mugsey Dogs, the Cottage shakers (this set had the "Essex China" sticker on it), and the five inch "Chanticleer" chickens.

Row Three pictures the smaller versions of some of the above mentioned sets; the small Mugsey Dog, Boy Pig and Winnie and the small chickens.

The bottom shelf holds the small fruit, salt-and-pepper chefs, and finally, the watering cans.

There are many other sets of Shawnee to find. They are made of a high quality ceramic. One can learn to distinquish the Shawnee sets from others, by the size of the holes in the bottom of the shakers. The holes are much larger than most. Once you learn about Shawnee, you will not only be able to pick it out from a distance, you will learn to love it!

The cottage set in the center of Row Two is a difficult set to find.

The chefs in the center of Row Four have gold trim; the price listed reflects this.

Row 1:	(1) $45.00-$55.00	(2) $65.00-$75.00	(3) $35.00-$45.00
Row 2:	(1) $60.00-$75.00	(2) $175.00-$200.00	(3) $40.00-$50.00
Row 3:	(1) $35.00-$45.00	(2) $45.00-$65.00	(3) $25.00-$35.00
Row 4:	(1) $18.00-$20.00	(2) $35.00-$40.00 (gold)	(3) $15.00-$18.00

25

SNUGGLE-HUGS

In March of 1986, the world lost one of its most talented artists, Ruth Van Tellingen Bendel. From what I have been told by friends who were lucky enough to have known her, she was a delightful person with a great love for children. Her warmth and charm were often expressed throughout the wonderful illustrations she created for several children's magazines.

The "Snuggle-Hugs" salt-and-pepper shakers were designed by her in 1947. As you can see, several different styles were made and most of them came in color variations. The earliest sets were impressed "Van Tellingen, Patent Pending." The sets which were manufactured after the patent was granted on July 17, 1951, are marked with the name and patent number.

In the photograph, all the sets in Row One are signed "Bendel" and all have the patent number. The first set is the Bendel bear. The second set, the "Love Bugs," is larger and the shakers are maroon, the only color in this size, according to Don Brewer's study. The last set in the row, the smaller "Love Bugs," is found not only in maroon but also in green and dark gray. The "Love Bugs" are not as easy to find as some of the other sets and therefore, the prices are generally higher for these sets. The larger set commands an even greater premium because it is so seldom found. I have also heard that there is a Bendel bunny which was released in 1958. This set, which is gray and white, would be quite rare and a great find for any collector.

I would like to thank Don Brewer for his help in documenting much of the information about the Van Tellingen shakers. He has worked many years doing research on these shakers and has been instrumental in bringing this wonderful artist to the attention of many collectors. In 1983, Don wrote several articles for the "Daze" about Ruth Van Tellingen Bendel and her work. He was at our 1988 Shaker Convention. So many of us were very pleased to finally meet him! Irene Thornburg, from our S & P Club and Don Brewer compiled all the material from Don's studies and made a report to hand out at the convention. This material will be treasured for many years to come; our sincere thanks to both of you.

Now...back to the shakers. When Mrs. Bendel designed these shakers, she invented new features to help the consumer. While it is obvious that the shakers fit together in a hugging position, what most people do not realize is that she made them in this way so that both shakers could be picked up at once, without a chance of dropping either of them. She also designed them with the holes on the same side so that both condiments could be dispensed at the same time by using only one hand. The bottoms of all her shakers are so balanced that it is virtually impossible to knock them over...all the ideas and work of a truly ingenious person!

All of the Van Tellingen shakers were made by the Regal China Corporation, which is owned by the Jim Beam Distilleries. Regal also makes the porcelain Beam bottle, another very collectible item.

The remaining shakers on the page are marked "Van Tellingen." In Row Two, the first and last sets are "Bear Hugs" and come in brown and pink, as pictured here, as well as in yellow and green and several variations of decoration in all colors. The mermaid and the sailor in the center of the row is one of the most elusive sets. It is only found in the colors illustrated here and, because of its scarcity, merits a high price. The Dutch couple, the first set in Row Three, also comes in just one style but is more plentiful than the mermaid/sailor set. Mary and her lamb are the second and third sets in Row Three. Although Mary remains the same in all sets, the lamb can be found in the pictured gray or white, as well as yellow or a very rare black.

In Row Four, we find a little boy and his dog. The boy can be found in white, brown or black, although lighter or darker variations are known. The dog has also been found in several variations. In Row Five, the "Bunny Hugs" sets one and three are shown in yellow and white respectively; the set also comes in green, pink and light brown. The accents applied have a great variety of colors which makes each set unique. The ducks in the center of this row are found only in yellow with, again, a variety of color accents.

Row 1:	(1) $100.00-$125.00	(2) $100.00-$150.00	(3) $50.00-$65.00
Row 2:	(1) $20.00-$25.00	(2) $150.00-$195.00	(3) $20.00-$25.00
Row 3:	ALL SETS: $35.00-$45.00 per set		
Row 4:	(1) $75.00-$95.00	(2) $75.00-$95.00	(3) $75.00-$95.00
Row 5:	(1) $18.00-$20.00	(2) $40.00-$45.00	(3) $18.00-$20.00

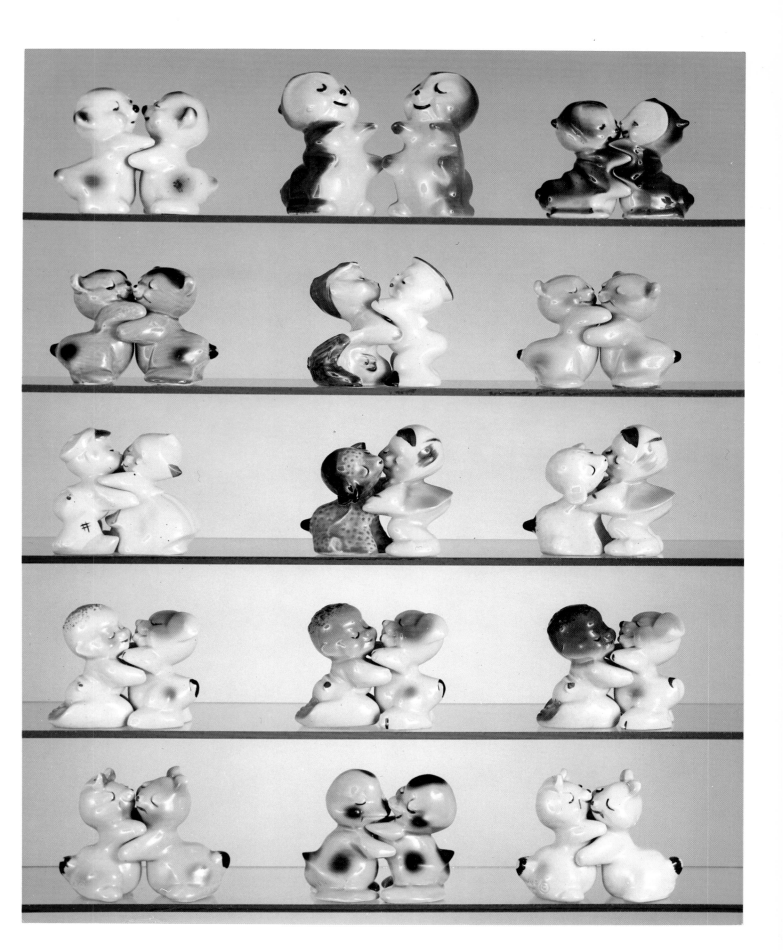

SNUGGLE-HUGS (continued)

There's nothing to beef about if you own this large set of Bendel Pigs! They are 6½" high. It is apparent that the same mold was used to make piggy banks, because there is a slight impression of the coin slot on the shaker. The color illustrated is the only color combination reported; there is, however, a smaller set of pigs which has been reported to be yellow and pink. The smaller set is marked "Van Tellingen." I would be delighted to add any or all of them to my collection someday.

Another set that would be heaven to find is the "Peek-A-Boo" set. It includes shakers that come in a large and small version, as well as a wonderful cookie jar to match...the only cookie jar ever created by Mrs. Bendel. The darling little animal---possibly a chipmunk playing peek-a-boo is dressed in white pajamas with large red polka dots and his paws cover his face in a most appealing manner. The pieces to this set are extremely hard to find and merit the high price attached to them. Regretfully, I have none of the set to photograph in detail for you...maybe the next time around!

I have included the illustration for the copyright application for a set of Kangaroo "Snuggle-Hugs" that were never manufactured. (This information is through the courtesy of that tireless researcher, Trish Claar.) How wonderful this set would have been--they were designed so that the babies in the pouch hugged each other just as the larger kangaroos do. This patent drawing is enough to make the avid Van Tellingen collector drool!

Made of the finest quality china right here in the United States, the "Snuggle-Hugs" are not only a wonderful area to specialize in, they are also a fitting compliment to the memory of an extremely talented and loving lady, Ruth Van Tellingen Bendel.

Large Pigs: $200.00-$250.00
"Peek-a-boo," not shown, small shakers $175.00; large shakers $375.00; cookie jar $900.00 up

Fig. 6

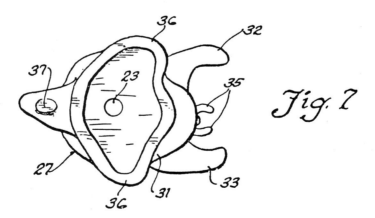

Fig. 7

INVENTOR.
Ruth Van Tellingen Bendel
BY
Kegan and Kegan
Attys

29

TREASURE CRAFT

The Treasure Craft sets were made by a family-owned company which started in 1945 and continues its operation today in Compton, California. All of the sets pictured here are signed "Treasure Craft, USA." A few sets can be found marked "Treasure Craft of Hawaii c. Maui."

Although I do not know if any shakers were made in stoneware, this company also produces a stoneware line that is signed "Pottery Craft." Since they often used paper labels to mark this particular line, stoneware shakers minus paper labels may be out there somewhere!

I think it would be interesting to collect all the states in Treasure Craft. As you can see, the names of each state are very easy to read. I cannot assure you that I have matched all the shakers correctly, but these sets were packed and unpacked so many times, I am just grateful to have them in one piece! When one buys shakers with multiple parts, it is helpful to note which goes with what--something I obviously didn't do.

Treasure Craft sets are usually simply painted in a wood-grain finish with a minimum of color. The exception to this rule is the chef set in the middle of Row Five. These shakers have a creamy finish, with a higher gloss and a heavier glaze than the other sets.

Although these shakers are rather plentiful now, I predict that collectors will soon start collecting them all. And when this happens, these easily-found sets will become scarce and the prices will begin to rise.

ALL SETS PICTURED: $10.00---$15.00

TWIN WINTON, RED WING, HULL AND REGAL

On this page is a sampling of some of the wonderful American-made shakers to be found. The companies represented here all carry a large line of items other than shakers. As a result, avid collectors seek not only the shakers, but also the cookie jars, dinnerware pieces and a myriad of other related products.

Since they are first on the page, I will begin with the Twin Winton sets which are the first and third sets in both Row One and Row Two. As you can see, they are quite large. The sets pictured were advertised in a 1965 catalog and are a Raccoon, Mouse, Friar Tuck and Butler. Incidentally, this is an *English* butler and not a black butler, as many people wishfully claim. These shakers all have matching cookie jars.

The Twin Winton Company is located in California. The name was derived from the "twin" brothers Ross and Don Winton who founded the company. A series of shakers entitled "Famous Lovers" were designed by Don Winton and are signed but, unfortunately, these sets are very difficult to find. The company opened in 1946 and changed ownership in 1977; I assume it is still in operation.

The sets in the middle of both Rows One and Two were made by Red Wing Potteries. The set in Row Two is called "Bobwhite." It was very popular when it was introduced in 1956 and it is even more popular today. Red Wing Potteries is responsible for many wonderful cookie jars as well as shakers. It is beyond the scope of this book to relate the long history of this company which began in Red Wing, Minnesota, but collectors will gain much invaluable information about this pottery as well as hundreds of others in Lois Lehner's book "*U. S. Marks on Pottery, Porcelain and Clay.*" PLEASE obtain a copy of this incredible book, the most valuable book ever published for collectors of American-made items. It will help you in more ways than you can imagine and I assure you that the initial cost of the book is far less than the price of stupidity, especially the mistake of not knowing what you have until after you have already sold it! Enough said.

I have included all the sizes of the Hull Red Riding Hood sets that I could find. The first and third sets are the most available, although they too are slowly disappearing with a concurrent rise in price. The second set pictured is almost impossible to find and is considered RARE. The set trimmed in blue at the end of the row is also rather difficult to find. *Anything* in the form of Red Riding Hood by Hull is highly collectible. Variety in the trim of Red Riding Hood items include a difference in the decals, the color and placement of the gold, red or blue trims, and of course the whims of the decorator. One could form a collection of just the variations to be found. The long and involved history of the Hull Pottery Company, which is located in Crooksville, Ohio, can also be found in Lehner's book.

Row Four includes sets made by the Regal China Company, Antioch, Illinois. This is the company credited with making the Van Tellingen "Snuggle-Hugs." All of the sets are desirable and their prices reflect this. The first set of Regal shakers pictured here is Humpty Dumpty siting on a bright red wall. A matching cookie jar can be found to accompany these shakers--a wonderful set! The second set, the farmer boy and girl, is part of the "Old MacDonald" series, released by Regal in 1949. The set includes all types of kitchen items made in the forms of farm-related animals, people or things! It is a set which is not easily completed! The last set is Goldilocks and Baby Bear; these shakers also have a cookie jar to match.

Many thanks to Carol Jessen and Betty Carson for allowing us to photograph these charming sets from their collections.

Row 1:	(1) $35.00-$40.00	(2) $15.00-$18.00	(3) $35.00-$40.00	
Row 2:	(1) $35.00-$40.00	(2) $20.00-$22.00	(3) $35.00-$40.00	
Row 3:	(1) $100.00-$125.00	(2) $350.00-$400.00	(3) $40.00-$50.00	(4) $50.00-$60.00
Row 4:	(1) $150.00-$165.00	(2) $85.00-$95.00	(3) $125.00-$145.00	

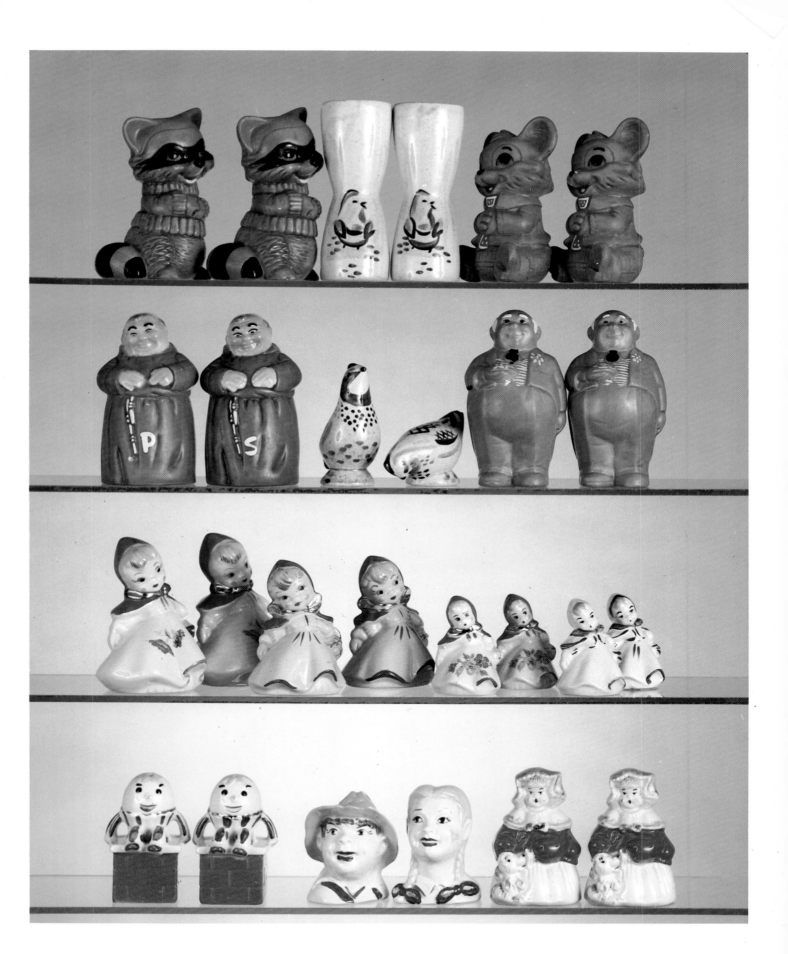

AMERICAN-MADE: MISCELLANEOUS

Those of you who may feel that it is a "cop out" on my part not to identify the shaker sets on the next three pages must simply bear with me. Until more information surfaces, I can do no more than guess – and guessing simply will not do. So I am extending an invitation to the American pottery collectors to share their opinions with us. Let me know what *you* think these sets are and I will publish the results of this survey in one of the pottery publications. I am sure some wonderful – and perhaps obscure – pottery produced many of them and I firmly believe that the collectors will help positively identify them all!

We probably all have a few of this type of shaker set in our collections. I wanted these sets – which are all out of my own collection – to be in this book because they are all very nicely done and of a pleasing quality. On the first page in Row One, sets one and three are bells and the handles hold the spices! Although I cannot positively identify these shakers, my guess would be that the Pearl China Company did them.

The bowling sets on this page may have been given at banquets. The first three sets in Row Five are porcelain and have decals from different colleges on them.

The second page has sets that resemble products from Pearl China or Hall China companies. Can any of you help with positive identification? The first set in the bottom row is done in "weeping gold," and several of the sets have a lustre finish.

These sets all have wonderful shapes and designs which should help to attribute them to a specific pottery. In addition, there is much fine gold decoration which would be prohibitively expensive to use today. In the 1930's and 1940's however, gold was used on practically everything, including salt and pepper shakers!

To continue with this group, the center set of birds on the top shelf of the last page is marked "Pearl China." I believe that the chicks on each side may have been made by them also. The candle holders are beautifully decorated with much tastefully applied gold. The sets on each end of Row Three may have been made by Kass. (Again, I will be looking forward to *your* opinions.)

Since I have many friends who collect, research and work with the products of American potteries, I have included this entire section for them. This is a large group of wonderful shakers that has been overlooked by collectors for too long. As we learn about them together, we will develop greater respect for them. Someone cared enough about these shakers to make them; others cared enough to buy them. Let us care enough to research them for future generations of collectors. I know the information is out there *somewhere* and I will thank you all in advance for your help!

PAGE 35:   All Sets on page: $8.00-$10.00 per set
PAGE 36:   All Sets on page: $8.00-$10.00 per set
PAGE 37:   Row 1: (1&3) $15.00-$18.00 set   (2) $20.00-$25.00
           Remaining sets on page: $8.00-$10.00 per set

ANIMALS: CATS AND KITTENS

The next two pages feature some fancy felines. The cat is so popular that it merits a club of its own (the address is in the reference section). Collectors of cat items usually have a miscellany. With so much to collect, however, it is often a good idea to specialize in one area. Many collectors have therefore chosen to collect shakers depicting cats and, since there are literally hundreds of cat sets to find, one could even further specialize in a particular type of cat shaker. One could limit the collection to only realistic looking cats or to famous cats like Sylvester, Felix or Garfield. These sets, of course, are not easy to come by, but they *can* be found and several sets are pictured in the Children's Section. Black cats also form an interesting specialty and are extremely desirable in any form. The easiest cat shakers to find are the cute but unrealistic or comic cat sets. Even these, however, can be great fun.

On the first page we have several of those "use at your own risk" sets, as I call them. I don't believe that anything which is covered with trim that could easily fall off should be used to dispense food. The last set in Row Three has rhinestone eyes. It would be unpleasant to say the least to bite down on one of these- or worse yet, be concerned about having swallowed it! The real fur on the set directly below is not quite as dangerous, but if you found it in your salad covered with salad dressing, would you know what it was or, more importantly, where it had come from? (You will perhaps notice that there is a small metal bell hanging from the neck of ONE shaker in this same set. Where did the other one go?)

The center set in Row Five has a squeaker device placed in the base. The squeakers work for a short while after you buy them; then they just seem to deteriorate and never work again. It may have made more sense to leave that extra space for salt or pepper since, as it is now, just the heads hold the spices.

The third set on the top row is china; the rest are ceramic and, as is so often the case, they were all made in Japan around 1950 to 1960.

Row 1: (1) $5.00-$7.00	(2) $18.00-$20.00	(3) $8.00-$10.00
Row 2: (1) $8.00-$10.00	(2) $18.00-$20.00	(3) $8.00-$10.00
Row 3 (1) $5.00-$7.00	(2) $8.00-$10.00	(3) $10.00-$12.00
Row 4: (1) $8.00-$10.00	(2) $7.00-$9.00	(3) $8.00-$10.00
Row 5: (1) $6.00-$8.00	(2) $8.00-$10.00	(3) $8.00-$10.00

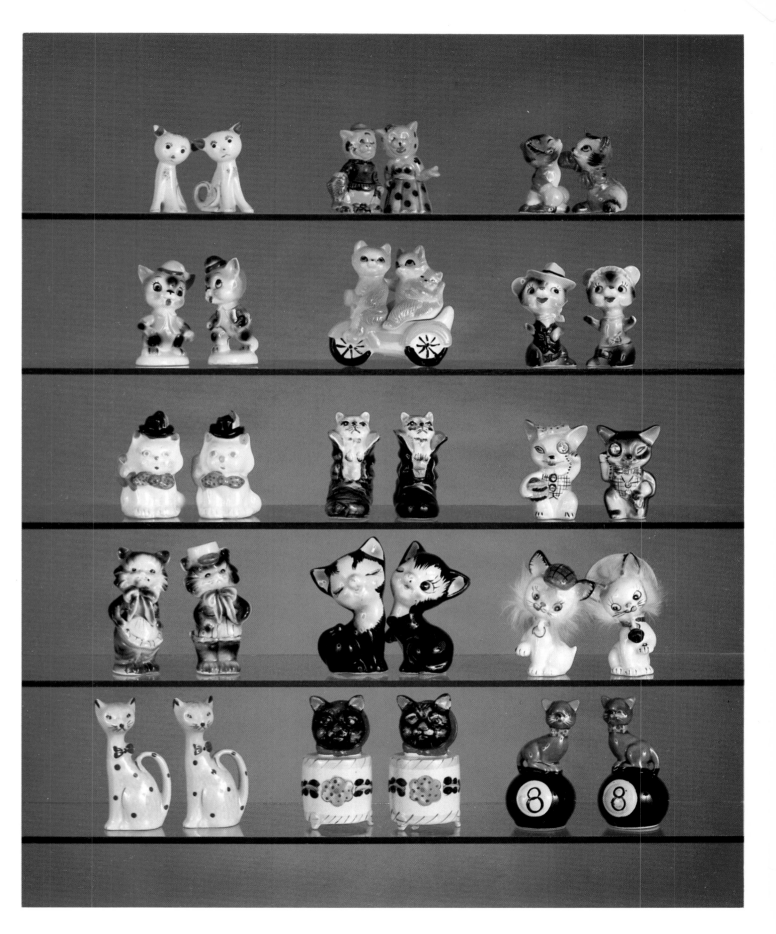

CATS AND KITTENS (continued)

On the second page of cat shakers, the first and last sets in Row One are teapot shaped cats! I have never personally encountered a cat shaped like this but this IS the world of novelty salt-and-peppers. Out of the entire litter, the sets in Row Two are probably the closest to realistic looking cats. The shakers in the middle of Row Three are known as "Playful Kittens" and they make a very nice set. The next set has REAL yarn to play with, a squeaker in its base, and along with the first set in the same row, wiry plastic whiskers! Really a utilitarian set!

The first set in Row Four is wonderful. It has a paper label marked "Poinsettia Studios, California." I do believe that this is where the shakers were manufactured, not merely its distribution point. The two cats are handsomely decorated with a fine over-glaze and they rest on an oval rug. If you know more about this company or have other marked sets, please let me know.

The last row consists of the black cats; this is just a tiny sampling of the variety available. I wonder if people collect them to disprove the superstition that black cats are bad luck. Whatever the reason, if one could collect all the black cat shakers available, he would have a most interesting collection. The center set is marked Shafford and is made from red clay, as is the first set.

With the exception of the Poinsettia set, all these shakers were made in Japan.

Row 1:	All Sets: $7.00-$9.00		
Row 2:	(1) $6.00-$8.00	(2) $8.00-$10.00	(3) $6.00-$8.00
Row 3:	All Sets: $7.00-$9.00		
Row 4:	(1) $30.00-$35.00	(2) $5.00-$7.00	(3) $15.00-$18.00
Row 5:	(1) $8.00-$10.00	(2) $12-$15.00	(3) $8.00-$10.00

41

FARM ANIMALS

The next three pages contain shakers of animals usually found on a farm. Of all the farm animals, the pig is by far the most collectible. The first page of photos in this section may give you some idea of the variety available.

On page 43, you will find an assortment of rather comical-looking cows and lambs. The last set in Row Three, which has been showing up more frequently at antique shows, is made of china and has gold-painted horns, bell and feet. The first set in this row is also china. The rest of the sets are ceramic and they were all made in Japan during the Fifties and Sixties.

The shakers on page 44 in the center of Row Two have the squeakers that never seem to work and the last set in Row Four has been made with real leather ears. If you unexpectedly found one of these ears in your salad, what would you think it was? Really furnishes some food for thought! The rather precarious-looking piggy back set is a lot more sure than it looks...it's held together with magnets.

The "Miss America" posing pigs in the center of the page and the last set in Row Five were made in Taiwan; the rest were made in Japan.

The third page of shakers is made up of horses, donkeys, and one lone goat with his cart in the center. Although collectors often prefer realistic-looking horses over the caricatures, I unfortunately had none when the shakers were being photographed. Donkeys, on the other hand, are always funny looking, as you can see, the horse heads in the center of Row One are very stylishly done. All of the sets with wagons or carts are very desirable, especially in this small size. Although they fit well into standard collections, they are even more fun when one specializes in them. These sets are all Japanese ceramics that were made during the 1950's-1960's period.

PAGE 43:
Row 1:   All Sets: $6.00-$8.00
Row 2:   All Sets: $6.00-$8.00
Row 3:   (1) $12.00-$15.00   (2) $5.00-$7.00   (3) $8.00-$10.00
Row 4:   (1) $5.00-$7.00   (2) $7.00-$9.00   (3) $8.00-$10.00
Row 5:   All Sets: $6.00-$8.00

PAGE 44:
Row 1:   (1) $5.00-$7.00   (2) $8.00-$10.00   (3) $15.00-$18.00   (4) $6.00-$8.00
Row 2:   (1) $6.00-$8.00   (2) $8.00-$10.00   (3) $6.00-$8.00
Row 3:   (1) $8.00-$10.00   (2) $12.00-$15.00   (3) $8.00-$10.00
Row 4:   (1) $6.00-$8.00   (2) $8.00-$10.00   (3) $6.00-$8.00
Row 5:   (1) $6.00-$8.00   (2) $12.00-$15.00   (3) $8.00-$10.00

PAGE 45:
Row 1:   All Sets: $5.00-$7.00
Row 2:   All Sets: $5.00-$7.00
Row 3:   (1) $8.00-$10.00   (2) $8.00-$10.00   (3) $5.00-$7.00
Row 4:   All Sets: $5.00-$7.00
Row 5:   (1) $5.00-$7.00   (2) $5.00-$7.00   (3) $12.00-$15.00

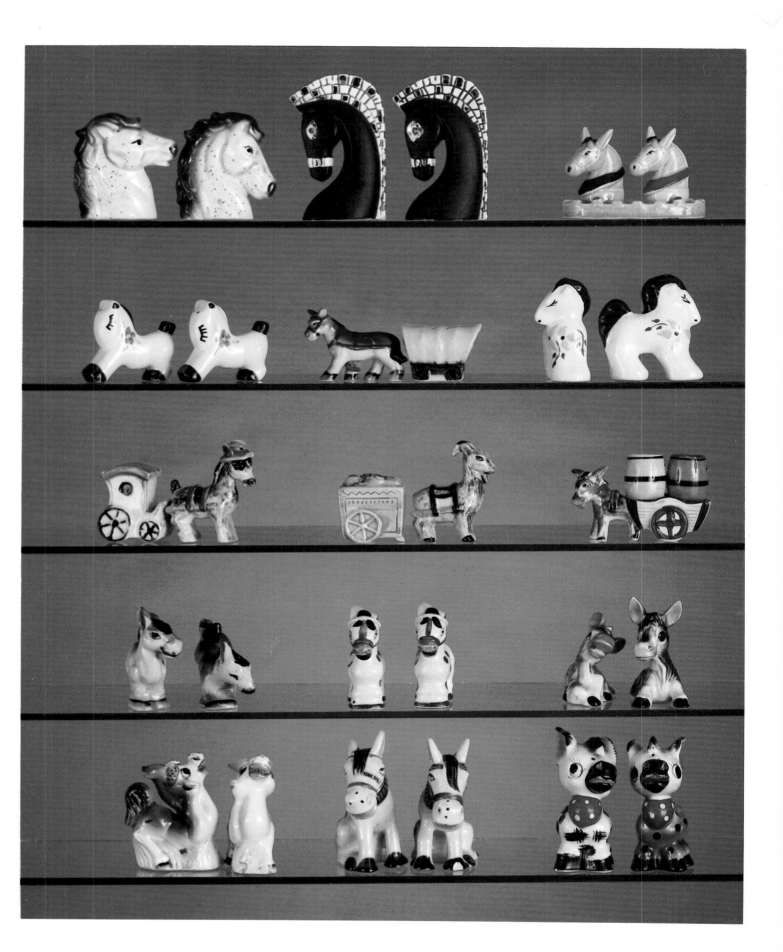

45

ANIMALS: HUGGERS, NESTERS AND LONGFELLOWS

This is truly a page of miscellany. The first row consists of Nesters and Huggers. Although the bone and the mushroom are on the shelf (due to the fact that they easily fall off when nested), the first and third sets are Nesters. (These are among the sets that need a rubber band to keep them in place.) The other two sets are Huggers and the shakers snuggle right up close to each other.

All the sets in this Row Two are by Fitz and Floyd, one of the newer names on the block. They have an entire line of shakers which are usually found in the better shops. In addition to those pictured here, there are a few more sets throughout the book. As I have said before, buy them as they come out or you may really have to pay dearly for them on the secondary market.

The sets pictured are nester frogs, hugger pigs and another set of rather constipated-looking frogs. (I know, I know – save the letters – frogs are not animals; these were just visiting!)

The next three rows consist of what I call "Longfellows," which must be at least six inches or longer. In the Animal Section a little further on, you will find their cousins, the "Tallboys," which are shakers six-inches-or-more tall. If dealers would adopt terms such as Longfellows, and Tallboys, etc., and use them on selling lists, it would be a real boon to the collector as well as the dealer. The entire field of salt-and-pepper collecting needs more standardized terminology!

I have found, incidentally, that the best way to display the Longfellows is to face them all in the same direction at an angle, overlapping each set about half the body length of the preceding set. They are great for either high or low shelves where you often lose the full effect of regular shakers.

All of the shakers are ceramic and were made in Japan, including the Fitz & Floyd. The first row dates from the 1960's to the 1970's. The Fitz & Floyd sets hit the market in the 1970's and are still being produced. The last three rows are mainly from the 1950's and early 1960's.

Row 1:   All Sets $10.00-$12.00
Row 2:   All Sets $14.00-$18.00
Row 3:   All Sets $12.00-$15.00
Row 4:   (1) $12.00-$15.00   (2) $8.00-$10.00
Row 5:   All Sets $12.00-$15.00

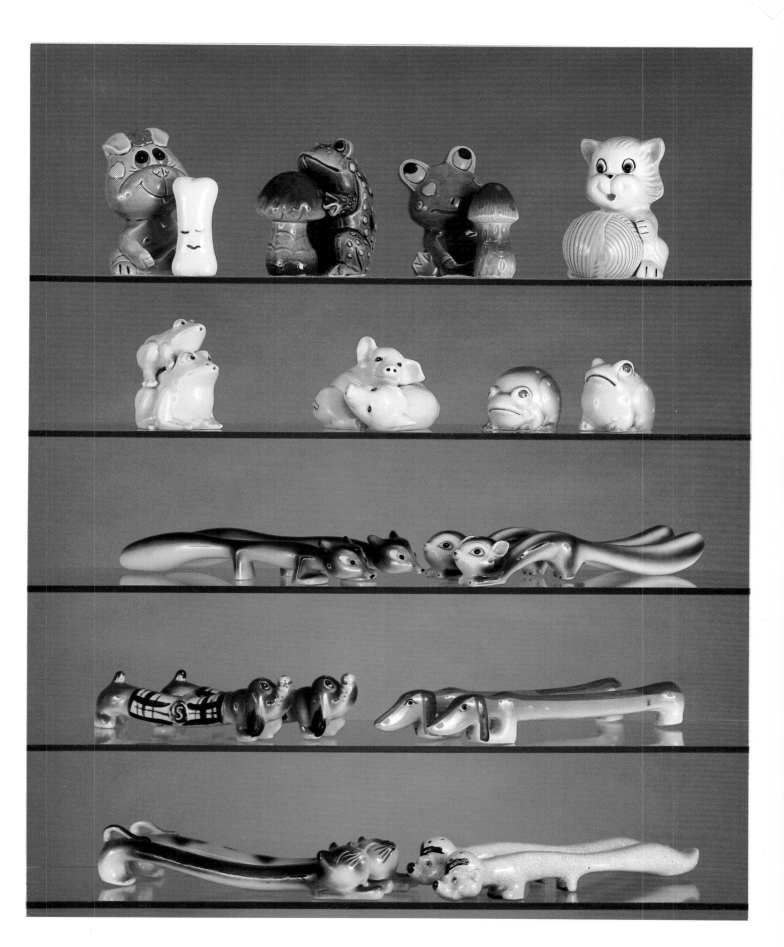

47

LARGE COMIC ANIMALS

Imagine specializing in this type of set – it would make a fantastic collection! Everyone likes animals imitating people. (I know a few people, of course, who do a good job acting like animals.) It is truly difficult to choose a favorite set from this page.

I will quickly give you a run-down on the plight of those featured here: the turtles are trying to figure out if it is going to rain; the dapper crows are waiting for the senior citizen bus to take them to play Bingo; the donkeys are having a few more horse laughs since the last book; the chickens have their feathers in rollers; the bears are going along with the crows; those wonderful frogs have just had lunch (this set and the bears are made of porcelain); the monkeys on each end of Row Three are watching the chipmunks in the center ice skate; the cute little ducks on the books are trying to be as tall as their parents next to them; the penguins are waiting for that Bingo bus; the cats in the center of Row Five are street musicians and the other two sets are feeling for change in their pockets! So now you know...

Since all of these sets seem to cheer up a collection, they are very popular with collectors and seem to hold a special appeal.

With the exception of the two porcelain sets in Row Two, all the sets are ceramic. They were all made in Japan (except for the bears in Row Two, which were made in Germany) from the 1940's through the early 1960's.

Row 1:	(1) $15.00-$18.00	(2) $12.00-$15.00	(3) $12.00-$15.00
Row 2:	(1) $8.00-$10.00	(2) $22.00-$25.00	(3) $12.00-$15.00
Row 3:	(1) $8.00-$10.00	(2) $22.00-$25.00	(3) $18.00-$20.00
Row 4:	(1) $8.00-$10.00	(2) $12.00-$15.00	(3) $12.00-$15.00
Row 5:	All Sets: $10.00-$12.00		

49

MAN'S BEST FRIEND

I must tell you about the selection of the dogs for this book. Just before organizing the shakers for photographing, I bought a collection of animal shakers. There were so many pairs of wonderful dogs that I just could not part with any of them. I even had my family help me to eliminate some sets but...as you can see, I still ended up with four pages of the most charming, delightful puppies one could find.

You will note that there are three cats alongside three different pups. They said that they were twins and preferred not to be separated, so I granted their request to stay together – although it did rather shock the canine world. These sets are the first and third sets in Row One and the second set in Row Two, rather irregular but certainly cute!

The dog in the center of the page is one of my all-time favorites. Made from red clay, he is dark brown with gold trim and an extremely glossy finish. Although he is not marked, it is possible that he may be American-made. No matter what his origin, he is utterly charming, especially with his basket just hanging from his mouth which gives a very realistic touch. I have never seen this set before, and if there are similar ones out there, I would love to hear about it...especially if the set is a marked example!

Possibly our all having been "in the doghouse" at one time or another helps to make the doghouse shaker sets very popular. Pictured are four wonderful examples to choose from.

The first and third sets in Row Three are nesters. I have seen sets similar to the dog-and-bucket set with different animals in the bucket. The last three sets are the ever-amusing dog and hydrant shakers. The first of these sets is rather unusual...he looks like he is arguing with the hydrant!

The baskets with the cat and dog in them and the last doghouse in Row Four are porcelain. The others are all ceramic. They date from the late 1940's through the 1960's. Sets one and two in Row Three, two and three in Row Four and the second set in Row Five are not marked. All the rest were made in Japan.

Row 1: (1) $6.00-$8.00	(2) $10.00-$12.00	(3) $6.00-$8.00
Row 2: (1) $12.00-$15.00	(2) $8.00-$10.00	(3) $15.00-$18.00
Row 3: (1) $7.00-$9.00	(2) $18.00-$20.00	(3) $12.00-$15.00
Row 4: (1) $18.00-$20.00	(2) $12.00-$15.00	(3) $12.00-$15.00
Row 5: (1) $10.00-$12.00	(2) $8.00-$10.00	(3) $10.00-$12.00

51

MAN'S BEST FRIEND (continued)

If this page does not warm your heart, you must not love dogs! I kept several of these sets for my own collection. Most of these shakers are very natural looking, which is the type that most collectors prefer.

The set in the center of Row Two is a pair of wonderful spaniels in a holder. Although it is difficult to see them well from the position they are in, they are beautifully detailed and would win anyone's heart with that "PLEASE...take me home" look that few people can resist.

The greyhounds in the center of the page are also very realistic – I would put my money on them any day!

In Row Four, there is a set of huggers on each end and a nester in the center. The nester is a three-piece set; the bodies are a one-piece base and the heads are the shakers. This set and the greyhounds are porcelain. All the others are made of ceramic. All the shakers were made in Japan with the exception of the black-and-gold spaniels in Row Three which are unmarked.

On the next page, all the sets are 3½" or less. This is a really balanced collection of shakers, with a wonderful variety of dogs approximately the same size, which doesn't happen too often. Most of them are hand-painted and all of them are Japanese. Sets two and three in both Rows One and Four are porcelain and the remaining shakers are ceramic.

The last page is full of fun sets. In the first row, we have the "glitter litter" complete with rhinestone eyes and buttons, too. Wonderful sets to collect but a real hazard to use! Poodle sets are always popular, possibly because they bring back such great memories of the "Fabulous Fifties" when poodles were all the rage. The black set in the center of the page is in a holder; the dogs, which are made of porcelain, have long exaggerated pointed noses. The set directly above in Row Two is also porcelain. The remainder of the shakers are ceramic and they were all made in Japan during the 1950's and early 1960's.

PAGE 53:
Row 1: (1) $8.00-$10.00	(2) $18.00-$20.00	(3) $7.00-$9.00
Row 2: (1) $18.00-$20.00	(2) $15.00-$18.00	(3) $8.00-$10.00
Row 3: (1) $12.00-$15.00	(2) $15.00-$18.00	(3) $15.00-$18.00
Row 4: (1) $12.00-$15.00	(2) $12.00-$15.00	(3) $12.00-$15.00
Row 5: (1) $8.00-$10.00	(2) $12.00-$15.00	(3) $8.00-$10.00

PAGE 54: All sets $5.00-$7.00

PAGE 55:
Row 1: All Sets $12.00-$15.00		
Row 2: (1) $7.00-$9.00	(2) $10.00-$12.00	(3) $6.00-$8.00
Row 3: (1) $7.00-$9.00	(2) $15.00-$18.00	(3) $8.00-$10.00
Row 4: All Sets $7.00-$9.00		
Row 5: All Sets $7.00-$9.00		

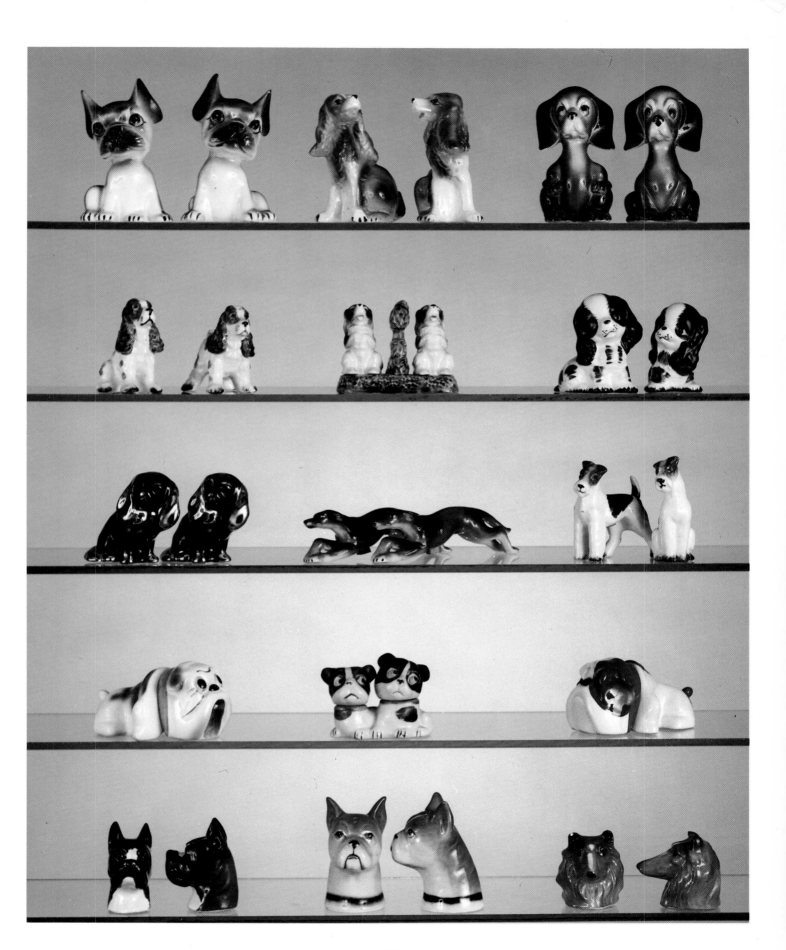

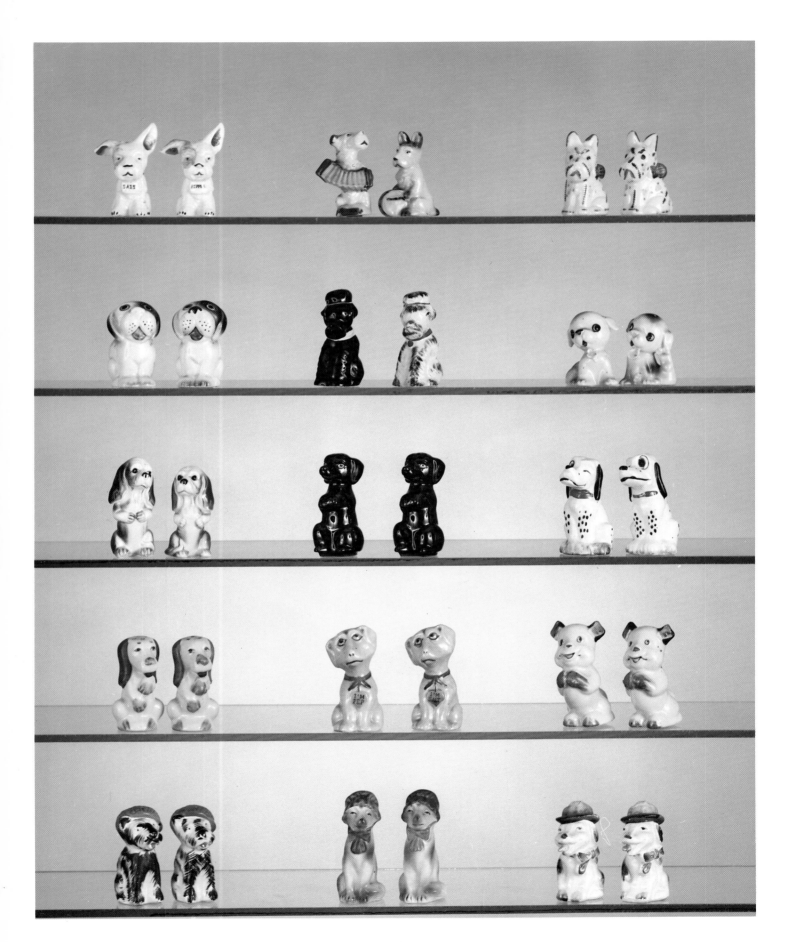

SMALL COMIC ANIMALS

This is certainly an eye-catching assortment of shakers! Animals all dressed up to "do" whatever little animals "do" is indeed one of the more popular areas of collecting. Most of the sets are hand-painted and, in the bottom row, are three of my favorite "use-at-your-own-risk" sets. They all have rhinestone eyes plus a few extras on the doctor and the cats – all adding up to a lot of glitz and even more fun. Oh, what sparkling spices one could create! "Doctor Owl," at least, is nearby to examine any victims (if his rhinestone eyes don't fall out, that is.)

All of the sets in Row Three and the first and third sets in Row Four are from the same series. They are newer--probably dating from the late 1970's. Each set has a name; "Rocky and Raquel" bears and "Oliver and Olivia" owls. How about "Sammy and Samantha" squirrels or "Fernando and Francine" frogs? It is quite a nice series, well-detailed and interesting and therefore a wonderful addition to any collection. Unfortunately, I don't know how many sets there were in the series.

The sets in the top row are the oldest, dating from the 1940's. With the exception of the series from the 1970's, the remaining sets are from the 1950's and early 1960's.

Although the second set in Row Two could pass for Goebel, it is stamped "Japan," as are all of the sets on this page. They are also all ceramic.

Rows 1, 2 and 3: All Sets $8.00-10.00 per set
Row 4: (1) $15.00-$18.00   (2) $10.00-$12.00   (3) $8.00-$10.00
Row 5: (1) $8.00-$10.00   (2) $12.00-$15.00   (3) $8.00-$10.00

TALLBOYS

Many people who collect the "Tallboys" shakers have a problem because it is hard to fit this type of shaker on most shelves, particularly those which were made specifically for shakers. It would be great if all the people who sell shakers would list any set higher than six inches as "Tallboys"; in this way a collector can determine whether or not he has the space to accommodate this size set. They do nicely, however, on the top of cases and, with so many different sets available, they can make a very interesting collection. Be sure to place them in the back of any shelf, however, because they can so easily be knocked over.

The third set in Row Two is made of wood. Although I try never to use a set twice, I added this one at the last minute to fill the page and I never realized that it was in the Wood Section until I received the photographs from the publisher. It is a nice set, however, and now you can have twice as long to look at it!

In another section, you will find the "Tallboys" counterparts – the "Longfellows," I think the name says it all!

Although it is a little hard to see because of the placement, the first set in Row One are green chickens. The stylized black cats are very "Felix-looking" but I don't believe that they were meant to represent that famous feline. The first two sets in Row Three are Napco, and the first set is dated 1956. In my opinion, however, the last set on the page is the nicest; it is made of a heavy ceramic material and quite nicely decorated.

All of the sets pictured are over six inches tall and, indeed, the shakers in Row Three are about 8½ inches tall. With the exception of the wooden set, all the shakers are made of ceramic and they were all made in Japan.

Row 1: (1) $6.00-$8.00   (2) $12.00-$15.00   (3) $6.00-$8.00
Row 2: All $6.00-$8.00
Row 3: All $10.00-$12.00

WOODLAND ANIMALS: RABBITS AND MICE

The first page picturing woodland animals consists of my favorites – the rabbits and mice. When I was young our family lived in an area surrounded by woods so we made friends with many of these little creatures.

I have several friends who collect only rabbits. They are all so cute and there are SO many to collect. I do believe the center set in Row Two was meant to represent Peter Cottontail with his little blue tail. The center set in Row Three is unusual because the rabbit, usually epitomized as being swift, is sleeping under a mushroom. There may be, of course, a slow-paced turtle behind the mushroom! The first set in Row Three is hand-painted, jewelry and all. You will find several sets of rabbits on the next page and a few more scattered throughout the book.

Another friend collects mice. She was probably as devilish as I was when a child and also carried mice in her pocket! The center set in Row Four is made of red clay and is known as "Dumbo, the Mice." I really had to check this set twice to make sure they were indeed mice. You will find a set of elephants, however, similiar to this set in the Zoo section. All of the mice-and-cheese nester sets are popular. I have only four of this type, but there are many more to find.

The first and second sets on the top shelf are not marked; all the others were made in Japan. The first sets in both Row One and Row Two and the third set in Row Three are made of porcelain. The black mice are made of red clay. The remaining sets are all ceramic. Most of the sets were made in the 1950's but a few may be from the late 1960's.

Row 1:	(1) $8.00-$10.00	(2) $8.00-$10.00	(3) $6.00-$8.00
Row 2:	(1) $8.00-$10.00	(2) $15.00-$18.00	(3) $5.00-$7.00
Row 3:	(1) $8.00-$10.00	(2) $8.00-$10.00	(3) $5.00-$7.00
Row 4:	All Sets: $6.00-$8.00		
Row 5:	(1) $12.00-$15.00	(2) $10.00-$12.00	(3) $10.00-$12.00 (4) $12.00-$15.00

WOODLAND ANIMALS: SKUNKS AND SQUIRRELS

Although they may not be so charming at a picnic or campsite, in a mixture of woodland shakers skunks and squirrels fit perfectly. One might even say that they have a certain appeal. Just look at that wonderful smiling face on the set in the center of the top shelf. Doesn't it remind you of the faces our children often have right after they have done something wrong? Makes you wonder what the skunk did! Some people will select sets of shakers that they believe are Disney characters. This selection of skunks will surely elicit a few "That's Flower from the Bambi movie," responses. Personally, I feel that if one chooses to add Disney look-alikes to a Disney collection, it is the option of that individual... It is also my opinion, however, that any official Walt Disney set of shakers should be officially marked, just as the Hummel collector would not collect Hummel look-alikes, or the Occupied Japan collector would not collect unmarked pieces, instead, insisting that the word "Occupied" appear on every item, so must the Disney collector be particular about *what he adds to his collection.* With all of the informative books published on Disney collectibles, one should easily be able to identify an unmarked item that may have once had a paper label.

Getting back to these particular shakers, however, is not a difficult task...even if they are not Disney. The skunk sets come in an astonishing variety and are, without a doubt, delightful to collect.

The last two rows are squirrels...another animal one can usually find in quantity. All of the sets are ceramic, made in Japan, and date mainly from the 1950's to the late 1960's.

Row 1:	All Sets $5.00-$7.00		
Row 2:	(1) $8.00-$10.00	(2) $8.00-$10.00	(3) $7.00-$9.00
Row 3:	All Sets $5.00-$7.00		
Row 4:	(1) $5.00-$7.00	(2) $6.00-$8.00	(3) $5.00-$7.00
Row 5:	(1) $5.00-$7.00	(2) $6.00-$8.00	(3) $5.00-$7.00

MISCELLANEOUS

This is a selection of raccoons, squirrels, chipmunks, rabbits, deer, doe, and a moose or two. All of these animals can be found wandering the woods in different areas of the United States. Although most of them are harmless, raccoons can be troublesome at times. I remember my sister-in-law going out to hang clothes one morning and a raccoon jumped out of the bushes, scaring her half to death! (They can also be a real pain on garbage pick-up day!)

The set in the center of the page DOES resemble Chip and Dale from Disney. Since they lack a certain "Chip and Dale" appeal, however, I would not classify them as such, but others may feel differently and add them to their Disney collections.

The rabbits in the baskets are made by Holt Howard of Stamford, Connecticut, and are collected by my favorite researcher, Trish Claar. The little yellow rabbits at the end of Row Three are made of porcelain, c. 1940, and are the oldest set on the page.

The realistic moose and doe heads on the bottom row are a nice addition to a woodland collection. The set in the center of that row, however, is quite comical. The eyes on the moose are made of plastic and are the type with the free-floating eyeballs that roll around as you move the shaker. Even when the eyes are still, they seem to look at you rather strangely! The Bambi look-alikes in Row Four are also charming.

All of the sets are ceramic and were made in Japan during the 1950's and 1960's with the exception of the yellow rabbits described above.

Row 1:	(1) $10.00-$12.00	(2) $8.00-$10.00	(3) $5.00-$7.00
Row 2:	All Sets $5.00-$7.00		
Row 3:	(1) $8.00-$10.00	(2) $10.00-$12.00	(3) $10.00-$12.00
Row 4:	All Sets $6.00-$8.00		
Row 5:	(1) $12.00-$15.00	(2) $8.00-$10.00	(3) $8.00-$10.00

ZOO ANIMALS: BEARS

I wonder if bear collectors know that there are salt-and-pepper shakers to add to their collections. I think that this assortment of shakers would attract any true bear collector, but I'm not sure we should tell them – the competition is already pretty stiff for these desirable sets.

Since there are so many varieties of bear shakers, both comic and lifelike, they are not only fun to collect but they also offer a great area of specialization.

The sets in the top row are rather large, but one would have to be large to lift weights! The mother and cub, in the center of the same row, make a lovely set; the mother bear has her arm around the baby and looks really protective. In Row Two, the first set is one of the oldest sets on this page. These shakers are hand-painted in a matte finish, unlike the mother and cub just mentioned, which have a highly glazed finish. Next to them are the ever-popular panda bears and, in the center of Row Three, is a very strange set made by Multi Products of Chicago. The set is made of wood composition and the eyes on these bears are very piercing. The shakers are dated 1948.

Bears and beehives are, of course, often found together and so we have sets one and three in Row Four, as well as the three bears in the center which would be a great addition to anyone's collection. The largest bear in the middle is attached to the base and does nothing except to keep the little bear shakers from fighting! The large pandas in Row Two are the newest shakers on the page, dating from the mid-1970's; they were made in Taiwan. The next set is from the 1960's and all the other sets date from the forties and fifties. All of the sets in Row Four and the last set in Row Five are not marked. I believe that they may have been made by one of the American companies. With the help of collectors around the country, we will hopefully solve many of the mysteries of the "here-and-gone" American manufacturers who made so many of the wonderful shakers we love to collect today.

Row 1:	(1) $12.00-$15.00	(2) $15.00-$18.00	(3) $8.00-$10.00
Row 2:	(1) $10.00-$12.00	(2) $8.00-$10.00	(3) $6.00-$8.00
Row 3:	(1) $6.00-$8.00	(2) $8.00-$10.00	(3) $6.00-$8.00
Row 4:	(1) $8.00-$10.00	(2) $15.00-$18.00	(3) $8.00-$10.00
Row 5:	All Sets: $7.00-$9.00		

ZOO ANIMALS: ELEPHANTS

Do you know how to get an elephant to follow you? Just act like a NUT!! I know these things because I have CHILDREN and they acquaint me with these facts.

Elephants are very popular with collectors and this selection would certainly make some collector very happy. None of these elephants are naturalistic; they are either comical or exaggerated in some way. Several of the sets are very beautifully hand-painted and the second set in Row Two has a lustre finish. The first pair of shakers in Row Three have brightly flowered blankets on their backs which are not visible in the photograph. The last set in the same row (and a charming set it is, too) sports bright blue overalls and orange shirts! These may be the gaudiest elephants in captivity.

As I mentioned in Book One, most collectors prefer elephants with trunks pointing up because many believe that an elephant with his trunk down brings bad luck. It seems that the first pair of elephants in Row Five just aren't taking any chances – their trunks are being held exactly at mid-range!

A few other sets of elephant shakers appear in the Circus Section of the Children's World...and, of course, we always need a couple of pink elephants, last two rows at the end.

All of the sets pictured were made in Japan in the 1950's. The dark brown or black sets are all red clay, the second set in Row Two and Row Five are made of porcelain and all the rest are ceramic.

Row 1:	(1) $6.00-$8.00	(2) $6.00-$8.00	(3) $5.00-$7.00
Row 2:	(1) $7.00-$9.00	(2) $10.00-$12.00	(3) $7.00-$9.00
Row 3:	(1) $12.00-$15.00	(2) $6.00-$8.00	(3) $10.00-$12.00
Row 4:	(1) $6.00-$8.00	(2) $7.00-$9.00	(3) $6.00-$8.00
Row 5:	(1) $5.00-$7.00	(2) $10.00-$12.00	(3) $8.00-$10.00

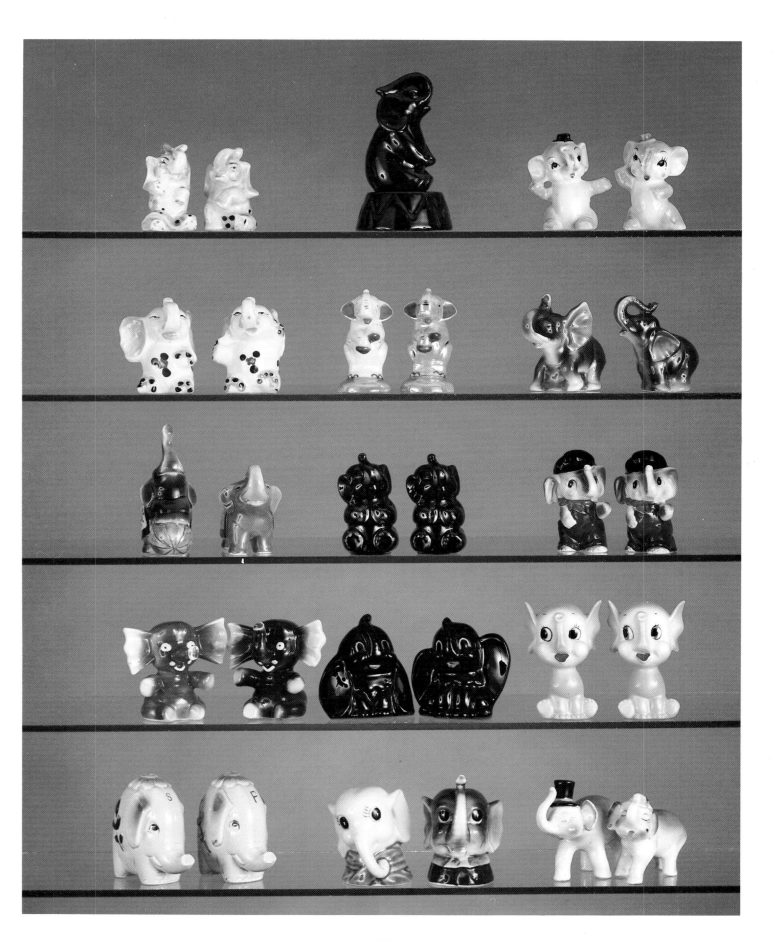

ZOO ANIMALS: MONKEYS

Have you ever thought that you may have been an animal in a former life? I think that I may have been a monkey; my brother Bill and my sister Dee, of course, would have been there, too! (I had to specify which brother and sister because the other two are rather normal...) The three of us used to swing from trees, and we ate loads of bananas and we loved to go see the monkeys at the Highland Park Zoo or visit the monkey cage at Kennywood. Monkeys are always fun, and so are we!

The person who said, "I'll have no monkey shines!," obviously wasn't looking for the guys in the first set of shakers on this page. They are ready and waiting with a five-cent shine. The last set of shakers in Row One, however, appear to be waiting for the giraffe from the next page; they must be meeting a few friends for a night out on the town. How gentlemanly he is tipping his hat as some folks ride by on their bike! When the subject matter is as amusing as monkeys, visual puns seem to proliferate – notice the monkeys in "banana boats" in Row Four! By the way, remember "Speak No Evil" from the last book? Well, I found his brothers "Hear No Evil" and "See No Evil" and they form the first set in the last row. Anyway, that's enough monkeying around! (O.K., O.K.,...I'll quit!)

The three sets in Row Five are porcelain; the remaining sets are ceramic. The monkey under the palm tree in Row Four and the last two sets in the bottom row are not marked, but I believe they may be American, possibly Parkcraft or Arcadia. Does anyone know? Please drop me a line if you have any information about these sets. Other than these, the rest of the shakers were made in Japan and most date from the 1950's or early 1960's with the exception of the first set in Row Five which is from the 1940's.

Row 1:   (1) $15.00-$18.00   (2) $18.00-$20.00   (3) $15.00-$18.00
Row 2:   All Sets $7.00-$9.00
Row 3:   (1) $10.00-$12.00   (2) $10.00-$12.00   (3) $8.00-$10.00
Row 4:   All Sets $10.00-$12.00
Row 5:   (1) $15.00-$18.00   (2) $8.00-$10.00   (3) $6.00-$8.00

ZOO ANIMALS: MISCELLANEOUS

Anyone who loves the zoo would be thrilled to have the selection of zoo animals pictured on the next few pages – if he is a shaker collector, that is. Zoo animals can be fascinating. Since I am only five feet tall, for example, the giraffe has always been of special interest to me. How could he be so tall and I so short??? No one, of course, has ever had to tell me to duck my head when I am going through a doorway!

Most of the animal sets pictured here are caricatures. The giraffes in the center of Row One are wonderful, all dressed up in suits and ties. Collections specializing in "dressed animal" shakers are always amusing, which is probably why there are so many people who collect this type of set.

The zebra sets are also popular but are not as easily found as most of the other animals. The pink-and-black zebras have an Art Deco flair to them – rather appealing. The sets in Row Three are hippos, another hard-to-find animal. Shortly after Book One was published, my friend, Irene Thornburg, sent me the set of buffalo pictured. I had mentioned that this was the most elusive animal and, as you can see, this is again the only set I had for this book.

The bottom row consists of kangaroo mother-and-baby sets on each end and boxing kangaroos in the center. The mother-and-baby sets are nesters, and are very popular.

The last set of giraffe in Row One and the boxing kangaroos in Row Five, as well as the Deco zebras in the Row Two, are all made from red clay. The pink giraffe, the first and third sets of zebras and the last set of kangaroos are made of porcelain. The remaining sets which were not mentioned are ceramic. All the shakers were made in Japan from 1950's to the early 1960's.

Row 1: (1) $6.00-$8.00   (2) $18.00-$20.00   (3) $6.00-$8.00
Row 2: All Sets $7.00-$9.00
Row 3: All Sets $8.00-$10.00
Row 4: (1) $10.00-$12.00   (2) $7.00-$9.00   (3) $10.00-$12.00
Row 5: (1) $18.00-$20.00   (2) $8.00-$10.00   (3) $12.00-$15.00

ADVERTISING

This is quite a popular area to specialize in, so look for some competition searching for sets. Also, keep in mind the prices on advertising sets are usually much higher than on common shakers.

The Blue Nun shakers are first in Row One. They advertise Blue Nun Wine and were available in the early 1980's. Apparently, not many were made, because they are not easy to locate and are in demand. The next set is "Snap" and "Pop" from Kelloggs Rice Crispies. It was made in Japan, not by Kellogg. Everyone asks, "What happened to Krackle?" This set was originally on a tray and "Krackle" was the mustard dish. This is quite RARE in its entirety. The last set in this row is Colonel Sanders; he, of course, represents Kentucky Fried Chicken. The same set was in Book One and was dated 1965. This set is dated 1971 and has a red base on one shaker instead of a black base as in the set in Book One.

When the first shaker in Row Two was produced, it was a part of a series of one piece animal shakers. No one has ever reported any of the others to the set, yet this does not mean they are not out there. My theory, as well as the reason the shaker is in the advertising section, is that I think the Exxon Company adopted this shaker to help promote their "Tiger in Your Tank" campaign. I recently found one of the shakers with "We Sell Tigers" printed on the side. Many tigers in all forms were use for this nationwide promotion in 1973. (Exxon was formerly Humble Oil Company.) The slogan was used as early as 1959 in just a few parts of the country. It did not go nationwide until 1973. This is about the same time this shaker was produced by Whirley Industries of Warren, Pennsylvania. The shaker does not have Exxon written on it. However most of the items used in this promotion were not signed Exxon.

The next two sets are replicas of old gas pumps. The first one is Sinclair Gas and the other is Mobil-gas. All of these pumps are in great demand, especially those with good labels. Many wear off through the years. The older and harder to find brands merit a high price.

The Greyhound buses at the end of Row Two are a different style than the set in Book One.

The first set in Row Three made its debut in the 1970's when the "self service" stations began to pop up all over. This is a nice set, although rather large. It only advertises "self-service," not a particular company.

The last set in Row Three is a favorite of many collectors. He is Lenny Lennox, dated 1950. It is an advertising set from Lennox furnaces.

The first set in Row Four is from "Trader Vics" and the last set is from "Kahiki." Both are restaurant chains, I assume the shakers were an *instant* souvenir from one of their tables!

The set in the center is special to people mainly from Pennsylvania. This is our own "Punxsutawney Phil." Every year on Groundhog Day, he sticks his head out of his hole and, if he sees his shadow and runs back in his hole, we will have six more weeks of winter. The folks in Punxsutawney really make a celebration for this event. I assume this is where the shaker set came from. It appears to be a hand-made set made by someone especially for this special event.

Row 1:	(1) $150.00-$175.00	(2) $55.00-$65.00 (as pictured)	(3) $65.00-$70.00	
Row 2:	(1) $12.00-$15.00	(2) $28.00-$30.00	(3) $28.00-$30.00	(4) $75.00-$85.00
Row 3:	(1) $25.00-$28.00	(2) $90.00-$100.00		
Row 4:	(1) $10.00-$12.00	(2) $20.00-$25.00	(3) $10.00-$12.00	

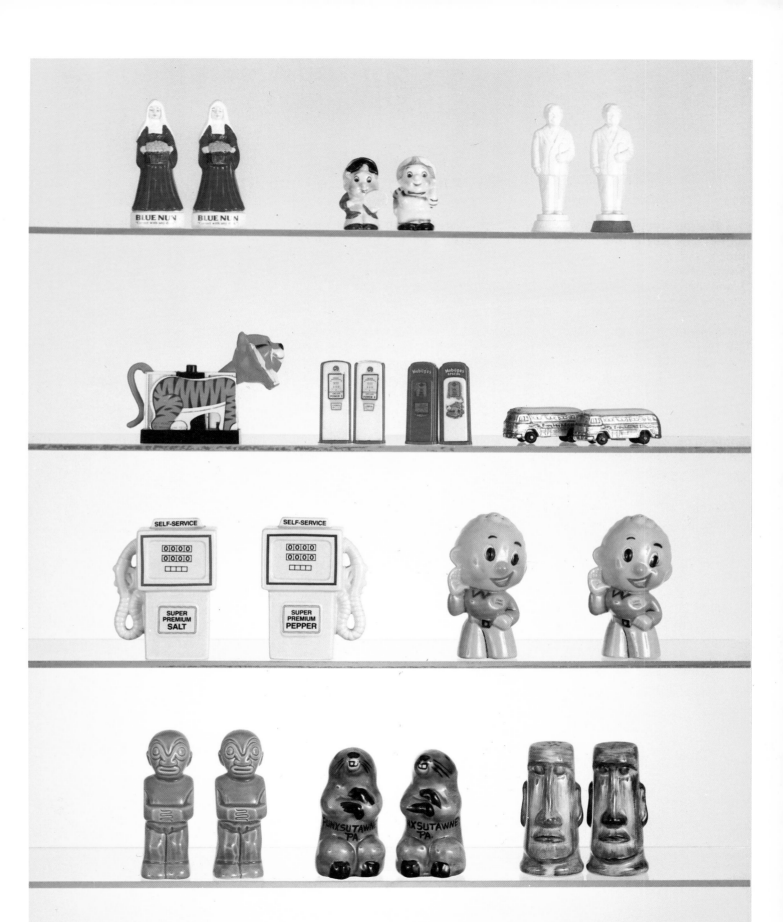

ADVERTISING: (continued)

The first set is an advertising set for a steam iron (guess where the spices come out!). It has no brand name. The set in the center of Row One is truly a super shaker. It advertises Tappan. The shaker is one piece and the spices pour from the sides. It is dated 1976 and is a relatively hard set to find. I did not know what section to place it in - Plastics? One-piece? So I thought this section was the most appropriate place for it! I included the T.V. again in this book because this one had the advertisement for General Electric televisions on the screen. This is the first one I have seen this way.

Combined, the first and last shaker in Row Two make another set of "Magic Chef" shakers. The set in the last book may have been patterned from this one. The set pictured here is plastic, but the set in Book One was crudely made of ceramic. This set apears to be the original one. I borrowed the "Campbell's" can shakers from Betty Zalewski's collection. It is a very nice set and clearly reads "Salt" or "Pepper." This set could possibly be from as late as the 1980's. I bought this set of "RCA Victor" shakers from a lady in a shop near Conneaut Lake, Pa. She said they came from a warehouse find possibly from the 1950's. "From your RCA Victor Dealer" is written on the side of the box, so I assume they were given as a premium for some type of promotion. The next set in this row is very interesting. The valuable information concerning this set is all written on the box, but "Who kept the box?" Sylvia Tompkins was lucky enough to buy this set, (after I passed it up!) and she loaned it to me for the book. If you have a set that looks like this one, turn it over and see if the words "Bride and Groom" are written on the bottom. If it is, your set was some type of a premium from the old "Bride and Groom" radio show. The box, in this case, was a super find. It dates from the 1930's.

I also included the boxes with all the sets in Row Four. Without the box, no one would know where they came from. The first is from "Stanley" products. We have all seen enough of these shakers in our travels! The next set is "Precision Sweepers"; however, in this case the name is on the shaker. The box says "A Gift for You." The last set is from "Stokely's." It is a pair of plastic magnetic, kissing strawberries. Again, if it were not for the box, it would just be another set of strawberries. This information is especially valuable to the avid advertising collectors. These sets otherwise would just be passed by. Unless mentioned, the sets are mainly from the 1940's-50's era.

Row 1:	(1) $8.00-$10.00 (with Ironing Board)	(2) $25.00-$28.00	(3) $15.00-$18.00 (with ad)
Row 2:	(1) $40.00-$45.00 pr.	(2) $12.00-$15.00	(3) $40.00-$45.00 pr.
Row 3:	(1) $35.00-$40.00	(2) $25.00-$30.00	
Row 4:	(1) $8.00-$10.00	(2) $15.00-$20.00	(3) $8.00-$10.00

ADVERTISING: (continued)

The beverage, beer and whiskey bottles are all collectible. The sets pictured are all shakers, however, it is not just shaker collectors who look for them, so it is a challenge to find many of the older ones. The center set of Squirt bottles is from the 1940's. The smaller set was used to introduce one of the new shapes of the bottles used by Squirt in the late 1950's or 1960's. The last set in Row One is from "Burton's Whiskey." This came with a shaker lid; however, people have taken miniature whiskey bottles of all types and punched in the lids to make them all shakers. This may not be bad to some people, but I must tell you about a collection I bought years ago. Some ingenious member of the family drilled holes in the tops of everything he could find in pairs! This included Old Spice bottles, all types of medicine bottles and, believe it or not, plastic toys and ceramic figurines that were not originally meant to be shakers! So for the sake of future collectors, PLEASE stick to the real thing!

I have included a few more mini-beers to add to the selection in Book One. In Row Two, the first set is "Piels, Real Draft," set two is "Koehler's" short bottles and the third set is "Schlitz" mini-cans. The first set in Row Three is "Barbarossa" mini-beers. The last set in Row Three is the tall "Koehlers" minis. In the center of this row is a set of "Coke" cans; this set came out in the early 1980's.

The "Heinz" shakers were bought directly from the Heinz Company here in Pittsburgh. I wish they would have copied the Hong Kong "copy" of the H. J. Heinz ketchup bottle and made it legal! We do like replicas of things! I bought the set pictured in 1987 for $2.00. I do not know if they are still available; however the price is always higher on the secondary market.

The center set in Row Four is another version of the "Pepsi" shakers. You will notice a difference in the logo on this set compared to those pictured in Book One. This set is the newest one. The set of lightbulbs is an advertising set for a lightbulb company. The socket end unscrews to fill the shakers.

In Row Five, the first set is signed "Possem Hollar" whiskey. I seriously doubt if this is a real brand! The next set is cobalt blue "Bromo Seltzer" bottles. The name is embossed on them just as the real bottles are. The next set is from "Oil City" glass company. It is very unique in the shape of miniature oil wells. The last set is a replica of the "Cathedral Ink Bottle." It is a deep red color. I have seen several other sets that were ink bottle replicas. These were made in the 1970's.

Anything with a brand name on it becomes a collector's item, especially if it is in the form of salt-and-pepper shakers!

Row 1: (1) $8.00-$10.00	(2) $10.00-$12.00	(3) $6.00-$8.00	
Row 2: (1) $12.00-$15.00	(2) $12.00-$15.00	(3) $7.00-$9.00	
Row 3: (1) $15.00-$18.00	(2) $8.00-$10.00	(3) $12.00-$15.00	
Row 4: (1) $6.00-$8.00	(2) $8.00-$10.00	(3) $8.00-$10.00	
Row 5: (1) $8.00-$10.00	(2) $10.00-$12.00	(3) $18.00-$20.00	(4) $3.00-$5.00

AROUND THE WORLD

I really wanted to make this section larger than just two pages; however, this was the best I could do this time. In the next book, I promise more countries and loads of shakers.

One country I especially wanted to represent with a lot more shakers is New Zealand. For those of you who do not know it, New Zealand has a very large and active salt-and-pepper shakers club. (See page 6 for club information.) I always find their newsletters refreshing and have made many friends there through the years. I do hope to get there one of these days for their annual meeting!

I want to dedicate this New Zealand section, small as it may be, to the memory of a dear friend, Rhona Day. She was one of my first contacts in New Zealand, she passed away in 1986. Anyone who had contact with her had the greatest respect for her. I feel very close to people I write to in New Zealand.

The first row of shakers are from New Zealand, all sent to me by friends. The first set is wooden and is signed New Zealand. The last set in the row is the Kiwi bird; it is not signed, but I am sure it was made in New Zealand. The center set also is not signed.

With too many friends to mention in New Zealand, I will just say to the members in Marlborough, Nelson, Levin, Waikato & districts, Christchurch, Hawkes Bay, Otago, Southland, Taranaki and Hamilton, find me some real New Zealand shakers for the next book!!

The second row of shakers is from Canada, all made there. We have several collectors in our club from Canada.

Rows Three and Four are all sets from Germany. Most of them are made by Goebel, the company who makes Hummel figurines.

The last row on the page consists of sets all made in England. I have had many other sets; however this was all I had when I was ready to photograph for the book. Next time, this section will also be better.

Collecting sets from foreign countries is a great area in which to specialize. It is really nice if you can visit all the countries and pick them out first hand! Some day!! A great help in finding these shakers is to have pen pals from other countries, with which you can trade sets. Believe me, they are just as anxious to find sets we find common in the USA. I have personally sent my book to collectors in five different countries. So the collectors are out there.

The sets pictured are from the early 1940's through the 1970's.

Row 1: (1) $12.00-$15.00	(2) $12.00-$15.00	(3) $10.00-$12.00
Row 2: (1) $10.00-$12.00	(2) $12.00-$15.00	(3) $8.00-$10.00
Row 3: (1) $35.00-$40.00	(2) $55.00-$60.00	(3) $35.00-$45.00
Row 4: (1) $55.00-$60.00	(2) $35.00-$40.00	(3) $55.00-$60.00
Row 5: (1) $10.00-$12.00	(2) $12.00-$15.00	(3) $12.00-$15.00

NOTE: I just noticed on the photo that the center sets in Row One and Row Five were switched, I recall now, due to the height of the set in the center of Row One. This set is therefore an English set. The set in the center of Row Five is an excellent set from New Zealand, with a map and all. Sorry for the confusion!!

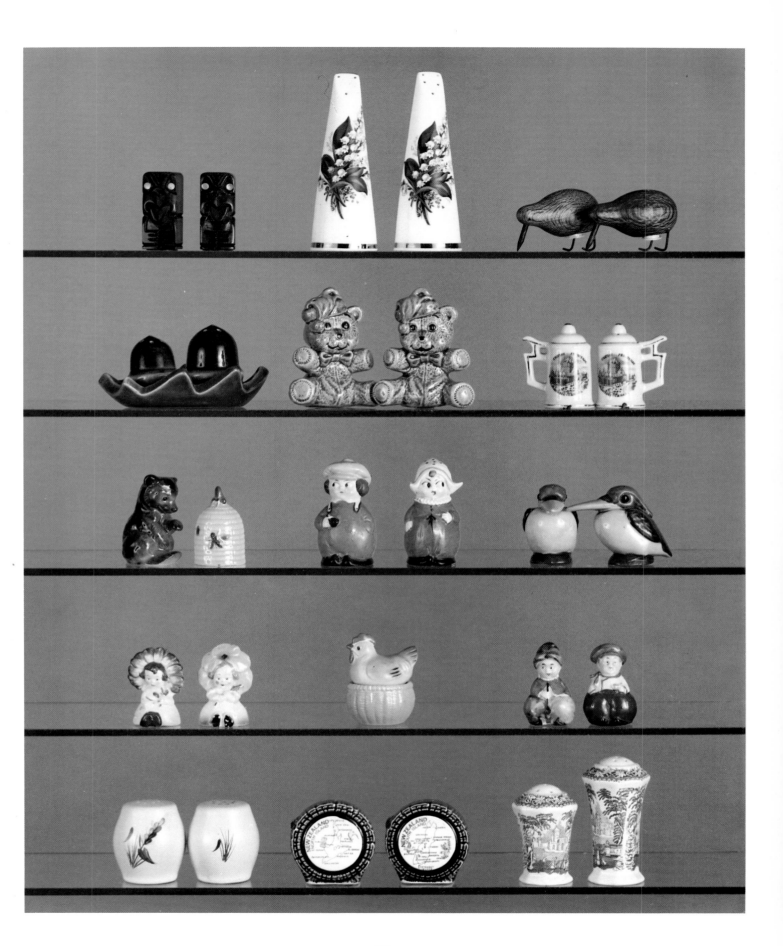

AROUND THE WORLD – MEXICO

At least I came up with one full page from another country! This entire page is from Mexico. All of the shakers were hand-made. The first three rows are rather crudely made, unique in the fact that no two are alike. The shakers are all made from clay and hand-painted, There is a vast selection of these shakers to be found. It would make an interesting collection.

All of the sets in the last two rows are wooden. The shakers were all hand-carved. Many of this type have very detailed and unique designs. All of the sets on the page are signed "Mexico"; however, the center set in the bottom row has "Florida" carved on it. I'm sure they were shipped to Florida to be sold as souvenirs!

It always amuses me to find souvenirs from other countries, that were made in Japan or some country other than the one you are visiting! We should be used to it, being from the United States; I think 95 percent of our souvenirs are imported. I guess when people visit us from other countries, they must feel the same way I do! I think I'll open a "Made in the USA" souvenir chain! (That is, if I could find the "Made-in-America" stock!!)

Well, judging from the selection of Mexican shakers on this page, there is no need for "them" to import shakers!

The shakers date from the 1940's to present. It is hard to date them considering they have made many of the same styles for years.

Row 1:   All Sets: $3.00-$6.00
Row 2:   All Sets: $3.00-$6.00
Row 3:   All Sets: $3.00-$6.00
Row 4:   All Sets: $3.00-$6.00
Row 5:   All Sets: $3.00-$6.00

BONE CHINA

Bone china is most commonly used in English wares. Beautiful cup and saucer sets have been made throughout the years and have proven to be a very popular collectible. The hard, white, porcelain finish originated about 1800. It is called bone china because the actual charred ashes from animal bones are added to the clay mixture.

The bone china shakers seem to be more durable than shakers made from other materials. They do not seem to chip as easily, or discolor as often as others do. Many of these shakers are still being manufactured today and are readily available; considering that porcelain shows little wear, it is difficult to determine the old sets from the new. Bone china items, including the shaker sets, usually have a small label or tag stating that they are indeed bone china, although a glance or two is usually sufficient to determine this fact.

Although most of the sets are solid white with a tinge of paint to highlight features, I personally prefer the shakers with more color. The owls in the middle of Row One have added touches of brown and black, giving them a rather natural look. The birds directly below the owls have shades of blue with a pink blush on their breasts, and both sets in the center row have added color to enhance their charm.

Row Four contains three rather unique sets. The tiny frogs on the toadstools as well as the minute squirrels on the tree stumps would be lovely additions to anyone's collection. The little rabbit with his blue-tinted egg is just adorable. Although it is a bit difficult to tell from the way they are placed, the first set on the bottom shelf is a pair of black-and-white Art Deco-type elephants which are very nice.

As you can see from the stickers on the bottoms of all your bone china sets, they state: "Made in Japan." One would think that at least a few would say "England."

Row 1: (1) $5.00-$7.00   (2) $7.00-$9.00   (3) $5.00-$7.00
Row 2: (1) $4.00-$6.00   (2) $6.00-$8.00   (3) $4.00-$6.00
Row 3: (1) $7.00-$9.00   (2) $6.00-$8.00
Row 4: (1) $6.00-$8.00   (2) $6.00-$8.00   (3) $6.00-$8.00
Row 5: All Sets: $6.00-$8.00

CHALKWARE

The fact that chalkware sets chip, crack and crumble quite easily may explain the fact that these simply do not have great deal of "collector appeal." In spite of this, however, most of us have at least one or two sets in our personal collections. In the world of shakers, there is always just one more set that catches your eye – even if it does happen to be chalkware!

If you have any of the old character sets in your collection, consider yourself to be very lucky. This series, made in the late thirties and early forties, consisted of sets such as Maggie and Jiggs, Orphan Annie and Sandy, Snuffy Smith and Barney Google to name a few. These sets are easy to recognize and first-class to own since they command the highest prices in chalkware. I'm sorry that I have none to show you in this book.

Included in the sampling of shakers pictured here, however, are three sets of bears in Row One. The first and third sets are rather nicely done and date, I am sure, from the latter years of chalkware production c. 1950. In the center of the next shelf is a pair of ghastly looking pigs – even making them look like clowns couldn't help these poor creatures! The fish, the last set in Row Three, appear to have been repainted. There are several sets of appealing dogs, although it does look as if they attacked the cats when no one was looking! The first set on the bottom shelf has an unusual texture...again one I am sure was used in the later years. The last set is the elusive buffalo, an unusual subject for shakers.

As I have stated, most people do not collect chalkware shakers, not on purpose, at least. In all fairness, however, I must also say that there *are* a few people who specialize in just this type of shaker. (Write me if you collect them...have I got a deal for *you!*)

Row 1: (1) $6.00-$8.00   (2) $5.00-$7.00   (3) $5.00-$7.00
Row 2: All Sets: $5.00-$7.00
Row 3: All Sets: $4.00-$6.00
Row 4: All Sets: $5.00-$7.00
Row 5: All Sets: $5.00-$7.00

THE CHILDREN'S WORLD

This is not only one of the most popular collecting areas, it is also the most difficult to price. Some collectors will pay almost anything for a set they do not have. In too many cases, the set is not even nearly worth the price paid for it. I have tried to hit a happy medium on prices listed. One rule still applies- if you want the set and can afford the price, by all means buy it! We do our best with price guides; however, we will never make everyone happy!

The first set in Row One is Pinocchio and his girlfriend, first in line. This set is heavy porcelain, the same as the set in Book One. It was made in Japan, where he apparently kept his girlfriend, since she was never written into the American version of Pinocchio! The second set is Popeye and Olive Oyl. It is a lightweight ceramic, made by Vandor Imports in 1980. Although Vandor is located in San Francisco, the shakers are made in Japan. The last set in this row is Donald Duck. This is a Dan Brechner creation. I must say his sets are the most collectible and are the hardest to find. They were produced in the early 1960's. Several series of wonderful sets were made. The first and last sets are Disney.

In Row Two, the first set is Disney's Donald Duck again. However, this set was made by Leeds China, in the late 1940's. In Book One, page 55, all the sets in Row Two and Row Three are Leeds China. At the time of writing Book One there was a lot of confusion as to who really did make them. Leeds China was licensed to make Disney sets from 1944 to 1954: they produced most of the shakers for Disney; however, they are not marked Leeds. In order to recognize them, you must study the style and heavy porcelain body.

The Bambi set in the center of Row Two, is a Disney knock-off, made in Japan. It is a good replica of Bambi and is included with many Disney collections. The Raggedy Ann and Andy set is made of light weight ceramic, 1970's vintage, Japan.

The first set in Row Three is one of the many versions of the rabbit and the tortoise, USA-made. The next set is hard to find. It is the Three Men in the Tub. The men on each end are the shakers, the man in the center is attaches to the lid of the tub, which is a sugar bowl. The last set is Tinkerbell sitting on a flower. The last two sets are Japanese.
Row Four consists of variations of the Cat and Fiddle. There are many others to be found. The center set is Japanese; the other two are American, unsigned.

The bottom row is made up of Humpty Dumpty sets. There are many other versions of this set to find, as well. All the sets are American-made in this row. The plastic sets in the center come in several color variations. I always felt these were offered to advertise something; however, I have not been able to confirm this feeling. I would appreciate any information concerning where this set originated.

Good luck to all of you trying to locate many of the sets in this section!

Row 1:	(1) $95.00-$100.00	(2) $45.00-$50.00	(3) $95.00-$100.00	
Row 2:	(1) $85.00-$90.00	(2) $15.00-$20.00	(3) $22.00-$25.00	
Row 3:	(1) $15.00-$18.00	(2) $65.00-$75.00	(3) $22.00-$25.00	
Row 4:	(1) $18.00-$20.00	(2) $22.00-$25.00	(3) $18.00-$20.00	
Row 5:	(1) $12.00-$15.00	(2) $12.00-$15.00	(3) $12.00-$15.00	(4) $15.00-$18.00

CHILDREN'S WORLD: (continued)

My thanks to Betty Carson, Carol Jessen and Betsy Zalewski for the loan of the shakers for this page. The first set on the page is a Japanese knock-off of Donald and Daisy. It is a porcelain set, very nicely done. The next set is another wonderful creation by Dan Brechner, of Mickey and Minnie. Although his sets were also made in Japan, they are official Disney Production sets and are all signed. Both sets courtesy of the Jessen collection. Snow White and Dopey, last set in Row One, belong on a tray. It was distributed by Enesco of Chicago and imported from Japan. Although this set just consists of Snow White and Dopey, you should also watch for several series sets consisting of all eight characters. This set is Betty Carson's.

The first set in Row Two is Sylvester the cat. It is signed Warner Brothers. I believe it was produced in the 1970's. The next set is Woody Woodpecker. It is crudely made but very nice. There is a Walter Lantz signature on this set, handwritten as is the name on the front of the set. I have no idea as to whether this was done by an individual in a ceramics class or if it is an official Walter Lantz set. Any information on this set, please let me know. Both sets belong to Carol Jessen.

In Row Two, set three is Woodstock and Snoopy. It is a late 1970's Japanese creation. All Snoopy items have become VERY collectible in the past year or so.

The last set in this row belongs to Betsy Zalewski. It is of Peter, Peter Pumpkin Eater and his wife in a pumpkin shell. This is a great set, made by Arcadia of California. It is not signed; however, I found a set that still had the paper label on it.

The first two sets in Row Three also belong to Betsy. Pebbles and Bam Bam from the Flintstone's cartoon were bought in the mid-1980's, from "Bedrock City" in Custer, South Dakota. There is an entire city set up with all the Flintstone Characters as a tourist attraction. "Dino," the family pet, sits in the center of the tray and aptly holds toothpicks! The next set was made in Japan and distributed by Relco. This set is just one in a series of six nursery rhyme characters. The set pictured is Goldilocks. In Book One, page 53, you will find two other sets in Row Two from this series. The first set is Red Riding Hood and the third set is Queen of Hearts. The other three sets (not pictured here) are: Little BoPeep, Little Miss Muffet and Mary and Her Little Lamb.

The last set in Row Three belongs to Carol. It is signed "Walter Lantz Productions, Incorporated" and dated 1958. This set of Oswald and Willy is part of a series. Collectors have reported mixed characters in different sets. This is usually the result of all the shakers in the series being on the same store shelf and the buyers picking the two they like best. Hopefully, we will be able to properly list the correct sets at some time in the future. The letters "S" or "P" are usually embossed on top of the shaker; this helps, at least, to pair a salt and pepper.

In Row Four, the first set is of Raggedy Ann and Andy. It is unsigned, American-made and very nice. This set is Betty Carson's. The next set is Donald Duck on a raft. It was made in Japan and is a super set to add to your collection. It is from the Jessen collection. The next set is Rock-a-bye Baby. It belongs to Betsy and was made in Japan, as was the last Nursery Rhyme set in this row.

The last row consists of: a pirate and his treasure; Paul Bunyan holding his ax with a tree trunk, (Paul Bunyan can also be found in various sets, with his famed ox, Babe.); the black bird sitting in a pie is a nester, as is the last set in Row Four, the Magician and his Magic Box.

These are all wonderful sets to own. They increasingly are becoming the most difficult sets to find. The prices reflect this fact.

Row 1: (1) $25.00-$30.00   (2) $175.00-$185.00   (3) $18.00-$20.00   (4) $1750.00-$200.00
Row 2: (1) $150.00-$160.00   (2) $75.00-$85.00   (3) $40.00-$45.00   (4) $45.00-$55.00
Row 3: (1) $45.00-$50.00   (2) $30.00-$35.00   (3) $175.00-$200.00
Row 4: (1) $25.00-$30.00   (2) $75.00-$85.00   (3) $45.00-$50.00   (4) $35.00-$40.00
Row 5: (1) $20.00-$25.00   (2) $30.00-$35.00   (3) $20.00-$25.00   (4) $25.00-$30.00

CHILDREN'S WORLD: (continued)

There is quite a mixture of characters from children's stories, rhymes and cartoons featured on this page.

The first and last set in Row One are of a devil and angel. I always felt that this set reflects the first thoughts of our children each morning. "Shall I be a Devil or Angel today?" This set comes in many variations. The stork holding the "new" arrival is a very popular set. Always check for broken beaks when buying this set. In the center of Row Two, you will find the church mouse with his church. At each end of this row are variations of the mouse-and-cheese sets and there are many, many other type sets to be found.

The first set in Row Three was made in Korea and distributed by Enesco. It is made of china and is 1970's vintage. The character, I believe, is Ziggy and his dog. The next set is another of Woody Woodpecker. This set also is very crudely made, unsigned heavy ceramic. The last set is Bonzo. This character dates back to the 1930's and comes in many sizes and variations. This set is porcelain and was made in Japan in the 1940's.

In Row Four, the Cow and the Moon, from "Hey, Diddle, Diddle" is just one more variation of this set. The next two sets are Japanese copies of Beatrix Potter's famous characters. The sets are very nicely hand painted and made of porcelain, 1940's vintage. The last set in this row is another version of the Goose who laid the Golden Egg.

In the bottom row, the first set is a knock-off of Warner Brother's Tweety Bird. It is a very cute set, distributed by Kreiss. The next two sets are made of chalk and are both Disney characters. The second set is Dumbo and the third one is Thumper. The last set is poorly painted porcelain and made in Japan. It is also Thumper.

All of the characters on the last three pages are wonderful additions to any collection. The collectors who specialize in this type of shaker, which incidentally is usually tied in with the advertising sets, always have the most interesting collections to look at. We can all relate to the many characters we have grown to love over the years.

Row 1:	(1) $18.00-$20.00	(2) $20.00-$25.00	(3) $18.00-$20.00	
Row 2:	(1) $10.00-$12.00	(2) $12.00-$15.00	(3) $10.00-$12.00	
Row 3:	(1) $18.00-$20.00	(2) $65.00-$70.00	(3) $10.00-$12.00	
Row 4:	(1) $15.00-$18.00	(2) $22.00-$25.00	(3) $22.00-$25.00	(4) $10.00-$12.00
Row 5:	(1) $12.00-$15.00	(2) $10.00-$12.00	(3) $10.00-$12.00	(4) $10.00-$12.00

93

THE CHILDREN'S WORLD: CIRCUS

I have extended the Children's World in this book to include the Circus type shakers on this page, and the toy types on the following page.

All of the sets seem to be performing in some manner. The first row consists of variations of seals doing the old ball trick. The second set is a nester, with the seal setting on a stack of discs. (I have seen the same seal with a different shaker; I cannot say which one is correct.) The last set in Row One was made by Harper Pottery, of California. It is very nicely made of quality materials. This set is qualified to become a part of Sylvia Tompkins' water-related collection!

All three sets in Row Two are nesters. The first and last sets come in an entire series of characters. The first set is signed "Shafford"; it was made in Japan, as were the other two sets in this row.

Row Three is full of super "action sets," as they are often called. The first and last sets are "nesters" since the riders are sitting on the other shaker. The boy in the center was thrown from his horse! They are all hand-painted and are certainly a delight to own.

In the bottom row, the first set is "Garbage Pail Clowns!" They were made in Taiwan and are china. The clown on a drum is a nester and has been found in several varieties. The tigers on a ball, last set on the page, are also very nicely painted and a great addition to any collection.

Unless previously mentioned, all the sets were made in Japan. Circa late 1940's through 1950. The Taiwan Clowns are later, about 1970's.

Row 1: (1) $15.00-$18.00   (2) $12.00-$15.00   (3) $8.00-$10.00   (4) $18.00-$20.00
Row 2: All Sets $28.00-$30.00 per set
Row 3: (1) $40.00-$45.00   (2) $28.00-$30.00   (3) $30.00-$35.00
Row 4: (1) $8.00-$10.00   (2) $20.00-$22.00   (3) $18.00-$20.00

THE CHILDREN'S WORLD: TOY TYPE SETS

There are so many sets that fit into this category, I felt they deserved a page of their own. I must apologize for not turning some of the sets more to the side. These are things that come to our attention after the photographs are done and it is too late to correct it.

In the center of the top shelf is a set of Raggedy Ann and Andy. This is a very puzzling set. I have talked with friends who collect and deal extensively with American pottery items. No one could help to identify the American manufacturer of this set. It is marked "Pat. Applied For." The set is very large and is made of heavy ceramic. The gut feelings of the collectors I talked with (as well as my own suspicions) is that one of three companies are responsible for this set. The shades of the paint use and the type of pottery is common in Purinton, Shawnee and Hull. We feel that one of these companies made this set. If any of you know, please let me know, so I can pass this information on to the people who have this set in their collections. According to patent information, supplied to me by Trish Claar, the patent was applied for in 1950.

If you look closely at the picture, you can see similiar sets; this is clear evidence that most of the shakers came in a series. There were also several styles to choose from.

The lions on each end of Row One form a most interesting set. They look as though they have movable parts; of course, they don't. They also have a rather stylized look. The set is very nicely painted and is a wonderful variation of the "Toy Type Sets."

Many of these sets have a hand-stitched look that greatly enhances their appeal.

All of the shakers in Rows Four and Five, and the set of rabbits at the end of Row Two are American-made. The remaining sets were made in Japan.

Row 1: (1) $12.00-$15.00 per set   (2) $65.00-$75.00 per set   (3) $12.00-$15.00 set
All remaining sets on page $10.00-$15.00 per set

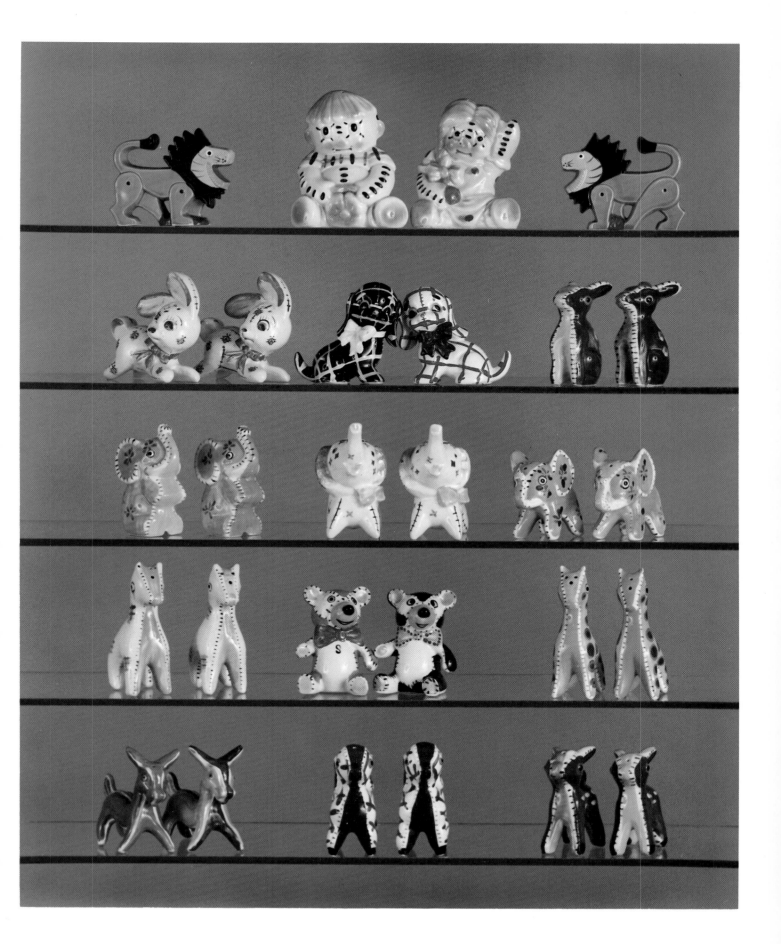

CONDIMENT SETS

There has been a recent upsurge in collecting "condiment" sets. This type of set will usually include a salt, pepper and mustard container. The mustard container was used for dry mustard, prior to prepared mustard being made. The dry mustard was sprinkled on your food just as any spice would be.

The most popular condiment sets are those with unique shapes of animals, people and things. The old Japanese sets as well as many German-made sets are the ones collectors are most eager to find. Although the English made sets usually conform more to their popular dinner ware lines, there are also some very nice figural condiment sets.

The first selection contains some of the nicest sets to be found. In Row One, the first set is a charming lady, which is part of the base. The salt, pepper and mustard all rest on the tray that extends out from the base of her skirt. The second set is one of the nicest I have ever seen. The little animal shakers hang from the tree branches. In the center of the tree, you see a small house, which is the mustard. Both sets are unique and very nicely hand-painted.

The first set in Row Two is also quite popular. The little koala bears are the shakers; one hangs from the side of the base, the other is the lid to the mustard. The train at the end of the row is a smaller version of the set pictured in the Transportation section.

The first and last sets in Row Four are among the most sought after. Both sets of dogs have a wonderful lustre finish. The last one is one of my all-time favorites. The dogs are attached and just the heads are the shakers; the base of the larger dog is the mustard, and the dog's tongue is the handle of the mustard spoon!

The long Dachshund in the center of Row Four and the soldiers with the drum in the center of Row Two are recent sets compared to the rest. They are from the 1960's. The containers with each of these sets are too large to be mustards, so they should be considered sugar bowls.

Both sets of lustre dogs in Row Four are made of porcelain. The sets were all made in Japan. Unless mentioned, the shakers date from the 1930-50's.

Row 1:(1) $65.00-$75.00	(2) $60.00-$65.00	
Row 2:(1) $45.00-$50.00	(2) $25.00-$30.00	(3) $20.00-$25.00
Row 3:(1) $10.00-$12.00	(2) $22.00-$25.00	(3) $20.00-$22.00
Row 4;(1) $35.00-$40.00	(2) $20.00-$22.00	(3) $45.00-$50.00

CONDIMENT SETS: (continued)

All the sets pictured here come on trays. The second set in Row One is an imitation of Beleek China. The beehive with shamrocks is a popular pattern. The last set in both Rows One and Three, was made in England. The last set in Row Two is signed "Foreign." This mark indicates that the set was made in Japan; however, it was exported to a country other than the United States. When shipping to the United States, all items must be marked in English, with the name of the exporting country.

The condiment sets in the centers of the first three rows, are all beehive sets, complete with bees! The remaining sets are all figural fruits or vegetables.

The sets in Row Four all resemble fruit bowls. The first set is made of porcelain and was produced in China. The center fruit bowl has two sets of shakers, adding a greater variety of fruit to the set. The apple in the center of the bowl is the mustard. The shakers in the last set rest in a rather elaborate basket.

Unless otherwise mentioned, all the sets were made in Japan. All sets are ceramic. The first three rows are from the 1930-50's. The last row dates a little later, around 1950-60.

Row 1: All Sets: $30.00-$35.00 per set
Row 2: All Sets: $30.00-$35.00 per set
Row 3: All Sets: $30.00-$35.00 per set
Row 4: (1) $25.00-$30.00   (2) $30.00-$35.00   (3) $30.00-$35.00

CONDIMENT SETS: (continued)

The first two rows on this page consist of very elaborate sets. All of them are porcelain. The first and third sets in both rows were made in Japan by Noritake. They are very collectible as are all Noritake items. The lustre finish on most of the sets greatly enhances their appeal. The center set in Row One combines a vinegar and oil set with the shakers and mustard jar. They all rest on a handled tray. The set was made in Japan.

In the center of Row Three is a wonderful cottage type set. Although England is most known for the cottage ware, this set was made in Japan. Besides being shaped like little houses, the houses are shaped into a teapot, sugar and creamer. And ironically, they will be used for salt, pepper and mustard! Imagination is what makes the shaker world so interesting!

The stacking condiments, sets one and three in Row Four, are great if you can do a balancing act! If your really like this type of set, take heed; there are teapots with sugar and creamers stacked in the same manner. I would imagine you could find those sets to match these!

The center set in Row Four was made in Beswick, England. It is titled "Circus."

Unless mentioned otherwise all the sets were made in Japan, circa 1930-50's.

Row 1: (1) $50.00-$55.00   (2) $40.00-$45.00   (3) $50.00-$55.00
Row 2: (1) $35.00-$40.00   (2) $25.00-$30.00   (3) $40.00-$45.00
Row 3: (1) $25.00-$30.00   (2) $55.00-$60.00   (3) $22.00-$25.00
Row 4: (1) $18.00-$20.00   (2) $45.00-$55.00   (3) $18.00-$20.00

FINE FEATHERED FRIENDS: COMICAL

Although, in my estimation, birds are among the most beautiful creatures that have ever lived, those on this page are an exception to that thought. They are instead the work of several artists with a good sense of humor. The purple ostriches in the center of the page are my favorites--they look like birds one could party with!

Set two in Row Two has a mustard jar in the center with the shakers on either side. Although not evident in the photograph, all three pieces are resting on a tray. This set is ugly enough to love! In addition to having strange little bodies and looking like fish, these chickens are also wearing clothing-and a good thing too, since they left for England shortly after they were photographed for this book. This set traveled along with the ostriches, the chicks emerging from the shells in Row Two, and the two tiny chicks on a tray in Row Four. These shakers are now all part of Nigel Dalley's collection. Nigel, who lives in Warwickshire, England, has graciously allowed us to use many of his sets throughout the book.

In Row Four is a wonderful pair of black crows that rest on a tray shaped like an ear of corn. These were manufactured by the Poinsettia Studios in California and, as is usual with this studio, the finish is of high quality and the set is beautifully detailed. Although several sets in this book are from this studio, it is necessary that they still have the paper sticker identifying them for, if the sticker is gone, one can only guess who made them. I do believe, however, that if one became familiar with the style and finish of the Poinsettia product, one would be able to identify the sets more readily. This is true, of course, of many of the American sets; learning what to look for always helps in identification.

The first set in Row Three, the chicks wearing daisy hats and finished in a rather strange gray-speckled finish, is signed Chivarz, California. Since I could find no further information on this company, I do not know if they actually manufactured the shakers or merely distributed them. The first set in the top row is unmarked, but I believe it is also American-made.

Needless to say, all of these sets are fun to add to one's collection. Unless otherwise noted, all the shakers were made in Japan. The mustard set in Row Two is porcelain and set one in Row Two, the chick coming out of its shell watched over by mother hen, is made of bisque and very delicately painted. The remaining sets are all ceramic and date from 1930 through the 1960's.

Row 1:All Sets: $4.00-$6.00 per set
Row 2:(1) $8.00-$10.00   (2) $75.00-$100.00   (3) $6.00-$8.00
Row 3:(1) $7.00-$9.00   (2) $30.00-$35.00   (3) $8.00-$10.00
Row 4:(1) $8.00-$10.00   (2) $7.00-$9.00   (3) $30.00-$35.00
Row 5:(1) $3.00-$8.00   (2) $6.00-$8.00   (3) $8.00-$10.00

FINE FEATHERED FRIENDS: FOWL

What a wonderful assortment of feathered friends for the sportsman or hunter. Sadly these beauties loose a bit of their charm once they hit the dinner table.

Colorful ringneck pheasants fill the first shelf. The center set, which is rather large, is softly detailed in a matte finish. The second row consists of two sets of geese flanking a third and very charming set of colorful ducks. The center set is unique, showing the full wing spread; in addition, the birds are perched on a box-like base with beautiful painted designs simulating a lake. The next three rows consist of a mixture of colorful turkeys surrounding a set of ducks in the middle of Row Four. The ducks have a matte finish and are painted in muted natural colors.

All of the sets featured on this page were made in Japan.

The next page carries a selection of ducks, geese and little chicks...all edible! In addition, there is a rather silly set of penguins in Row One, a set of pelicans at the end of Row One as well as several pelican shaker sets which fill Row Two. Since I have never heard of "pickled penguin" or "pelican under glass," these species cannot really be classified as fowl, but this was the only section in the book that they could comfortably perch! The ducks at the end of Row Four as well as the first set of chicks in Row Five are china; the remaining sets are ceramic and all of them are from Japan.

The last page in this group features every chicken one would ever want to see, and a few we could all do without ever seeing again! The first set in Row Two has a sticker with the name "Pico" on it. This was a company which was based in Los Angeles, California, known as the Pico Novelty Company. Although this company did do some manufacturing of its own, this particular set was imported.

The set in the middle of Row Five is from Holt-Howard, Stamford, Connecticut. Although this company also manufactured as well, this is again an imported set. Holt-Howard is still in business and has become one of the more popular names to look for when collecting shakers. This particular set has an Art Deco flair to it. Some people, incidentally, specialize in collections based upon the products of certain manufacturing or import companies-a rather clever way of curbing one's desires!

The first set in Row Five is a rather bizarre pair of multi-colored chickens with a textured finish--unlike *any* chicken I've ever seen! The middle set in Row Two is red clay; the first set in Row Two, the third set in Row Three and sets one and three in Row Four are all made of china. The other sets in Row Two, the third set in Row Three and sets one and three in Row Four are all made of china. The other sets are made from ceramic. Unless otherwise specified, the shakers on this last page were made in Japan.

The shakers pictured in this three-page grouping date mainly from the 1930's through the 1960's.

PAGE 107:
Row 1: (1) $10.00-$12.00   (2) $15.00-$18.00   (3) $12.00-$15.00
Row 2: (1) $8.00-$10.00   (2) $10.00-$12.00   (3) $8.00-$10.00
Row 3: All Sets: $10.00-$12.00 per set
Row 4: All Sets: $10.00-$12.00 per set
Row 5: All Sets: $10.00-$12.00 per set

PAGE 108:
All Sets on page: $6.00-$10.00 per set

PAGE 109:
Rows 1, 2 & 3: All Sets: $10.00-$12.00 per set
Row 4: All Sets: $6.00-$8.00 per set
Row 5: All Sets: $8.00-$10.00 per set

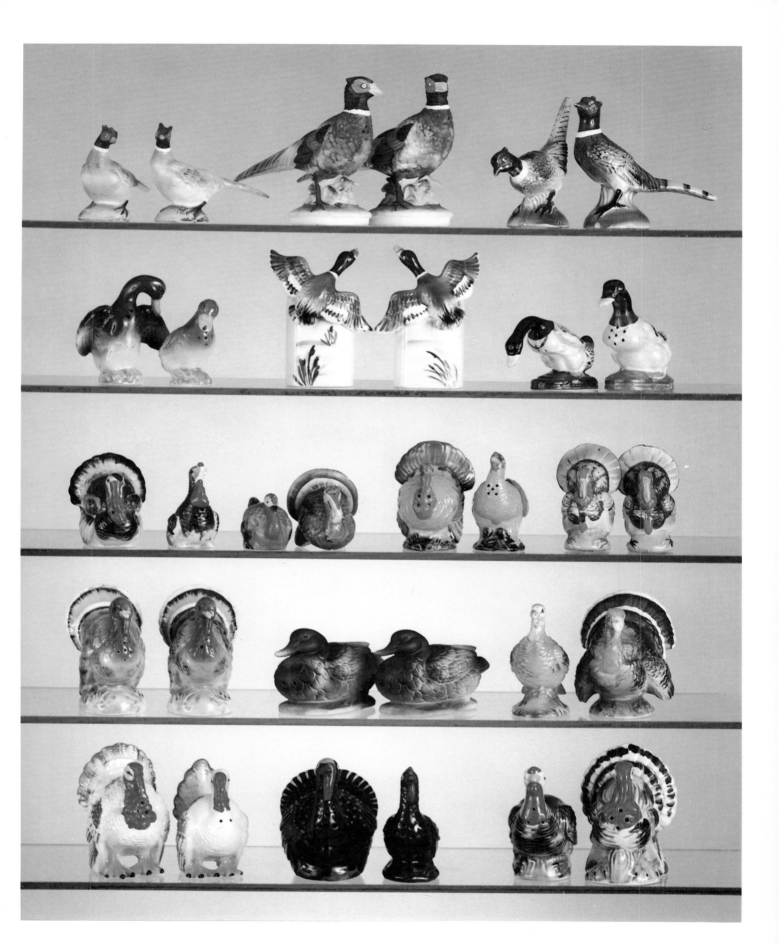

FINE FEATHERED FRIENDS: MISCELLANEOUS

The first set on this page was distributed by Enesco, an import company. The set itself was made in Japan and the bases contain those never-squeaking squeakers!

The second set in Row One was made by Napco which stands for National Potteries Corporation. This company, located in Bedford, Ohio, has acted as importer, distributor and manufacturer since its beginning in 1938. Napco usually signs and dates their products and this particular set is dated 1961. Both the Enesco and Napco sets have a lovely soft matte finish, tastefully decorated in natural colors.

In the center of Row Two is a set of peacocks, dated 1950, which were distributed by Murray Kreiss Co., importers located in Los Angeles, California. Sometimes shakers handled by this company are marked "Kreiss" or simply "M. K."

On the next page, Row One features sets less than two inches high. The remaining sets are no more than three inches high. The first set in Row Five has a lustre finish, a type now becoming very popular with collectors. Lustre is frequently found on the earlier sets from the 1930-40 period. All the sets on this page were made in Japan and are all hand-painted in bright, cheerful colors.

The last page in this group consists mainly of owls, the most collectible of the birds. The first set of owls in Row Three are made from red clay and are rather heavy. The next set is done in natural shades and has a matte finish. The last set in this row is bone china; a charming natural-looking pair to own.

The first set in Row Four is a set imported and distributed by the Lefton Co. of Chicago, Illinois. This company has become one of the most desirable names in the collecting field. The set of white owls beside the Lefton shakers is made of a rather heavy china and the last set is an an Art Deco style with a lustre finish which is quite nice.

The set in the middle of Row Five is very special. The larger owl has his wing stretched out around the smaller owl and they fit together, side by side. These shakers were imported by the Norleans Company.

To return to the top shelf, however, there is a lovely set of swans on either end with two sets of flamingos in the center. The popularity of flamingos seems to rise and fall every few years and, at this time, their popularity is on the "down side." Next year..who knows?

Although they have no name on them, the sets in Row Two are American-made. It is my opinion that they were done by the Pearl China Co. The gold trim suggests that, if Pearl did not manufacture them, they may have at least decorated them. Let me know what you think....your information is always welcome.

Unless otherwise indicated, all the sets were made in Japan, from the late 1930's through the 1960's. I hope that you have all enjoyed my selection of "Fine Feathered Friends."

PAGE 111:
Row 1: (1) $12.00-$15.00   (2) $18.00-20.00   (3) $10.00-$12.00
Row 2: All Sets: $8.00-$10.00
Row 3: All Sets: $7.00-$9.00
Row 4: All Sets: $7.00-$9.00
Row 5: All Sets: $5.00-$7.00

PAGE 112:
Rows 1, 2, & 3: All Sets $4.00-$6.00
Rows 4 & 5: All Sets $5.00-$7.00

PAGE 113:
Row 1: (1) $7.00-$9.00   (2) $18.00-$20.00   (3) $10.00-$12.00   (4) $7.00-$9.00
Row 2: (1) $12.00-$15.00   (2) $12.00-$15.00
Row 3: All Sets: $7.00-$9.00
Row 4: (1) $6.00-$8.00   (2) $7.00-$9.00   (3) $12.00-$15.00
Row 5: (1) $6.00-$8.00   (2) $12.00-$15.00   (3) $5.00-$7.00

FRUIT AND VEGETABLES

A creative collector could certainly make a wonderful fruit bowl display from this assortment of shakers. Just remember to warn the children not to bite into the realistic ceramic apples! There are literally hundreds of pairs of shakers that fit into this category depicting every fruit and vegetable known to man.

With the exception of the center set on the top shelf which is porcelain and which was made in China, all of the sets pictured are ceramic. As you can see, the tray sets are very popular but they are too often found without the trays. When Book One was published, I received several letters from collectors concerning sets that they had which were on trays, although I had pictured the same sets without any trays. So many trays have been lost through the years and quite often similar sets were made that did not include a tray; sometimes we simply do not know...and we have no really accurate way of finding out. So keep those letters and photos coming – sometimes the collector is not only the last resort, he is the best!

Although all of the fruit in the photograph is nicely done, none are quite as realistic as the peaches which are actually coated with fuzz! This is the kind of peach that caused me to fall out of the peach tree. Trying to eat with one hand and scratch "peach fuzz itch" with the other is not recommended, especially while still sitting in the tree.

The last set in the center row was sold by Avon in 1984. This set did not contain a product as did many of the sets pictured in Book One. There were not enough Avon sets made since my first book to merit another full page. Maybe next time...

The sets featuring heads made out of oranges and mushrooms are always bright additions to collections. Row Five has a small selection of vegetables, but the potatoes in the center are so realistic that I may use them for an April Fool's joke!

With the exception of the fruit basket in Row One which was made in China and the Avon set which is unmarked, all the sets were made in Japan.

Row 1:   All Sets: $10.00-$12.00
Row 2:   All Sets: $5.00-$7.00
Row 3:   (1) $6.00-$8.00   (2) $5.00-$7.00   (3) $10.00-$12.00
Row 4:   (1) $4.00-$6.00   (2) $20.00-$25.00   (3) $10.00-$12.00
Row 5:   (1) $3.00-$5.00   (2) $5.00-$7.00   (3) $3.00-$5.00

JAPANESE DECORATIVE SHAKERS

The next three pages consist of beautifully hand decorated shakers, all made in Japan. Most of us have several of this type in our collections; however, there has been very little said about them, mainly because they are not figural in most cases. Well, I feel they deserve some recognition, so here they are!

In Row One, the first and third sets are signed "Nippon." This mark was discontinued in 1921, to comply with the McKinley Tariff Act. All items exported to the United States, under this law, had to have the name of the exporting country marked in English. So since the word "Nippon" is the Japanese word for "Japan," it had to be changed to Japan, therefore ending the "Nippon Era." All Nippon items are collectible and the prices continually rise. As with the "Occupied Japan" items, many sets that were originally on trays are only marked "Japan" or have no mark at all and are not classified as Nippon without the proper markings.

The set in the center of Row One is signed "Noritake." This also is very highly collectible. The name has been used on wares since 1918. The name is still used today; however, although all of the items produced by Noritake are collectible, the pre-1940 items are the most sought after. Excellent books on Nippon and Noritake have been written by Joan F. Van Patten and are certainly worth the investment.

The remaining sets on the page are simply beautiful hand-painted table shakers, although I do believe some of them may have had one of those all important trays that would make them Nippon or Noritake, without the "marked" tray, they are just Japan. Take special notice of the detail in the last two rows of shakers.

The shakers in Row One of the next page, are certainly works of art. Moriage is a Japanese art, all done by hand. Many wonderful designs can be found. No matter how many items you may find decorated in the Moriage method, you will never find two identical. This is a very highly collectible area and I expect to see the prices for these items rise very high in the coming years. So, if you have any interest at all in the Moriage sets, grab them now, I assure you they will soon disappear from the market. This is one of the lost arts, another victim of automation. The remaining sets on this page are smaller than those on the first page; however, they are just as nicely decorated. Again, any of these could have been on trays marked "Nippon" or "Noritake" making them not only more desirable, but also more valuable. If you find the books on Nippon or Noritake, it pays to study them well; you may find a set you know has a tray and with a little persistence, you may be able to find the matching tray.

In the first row of the last page you will find three very beautiful high quality sets. I do believe the first and third sets are unmarked Nippon. The center set is marked "Japan." All of the sets in Row Two are delicately painted. The lustre finish on many of the sets on all three pages adds to their desirability.

The first set in Row Four is a Geisha Girl design. Every different scene has a name and there are many different ones to be found. This also is a very highly collectible area. There is a book dedicated entirely to Geisha Girl items, which is very helpful in learning the different designs.

The center set in Row Four is a glass shaker with a beautiful hand-painted design. All the sets range from as early as 1918 to about the mid 1950's.

PAGE 117:
Row 1: All Sets: $35.00-$40.00
Remaining Sets on page: $15.00-$25.00 per set

PAGE 118:
Row 1: All Sets: $28.00-$35.00
Remaining Sets on page: $10.00-$18.00 per set

PAGE 119:
Row 1: All Sets: $35.00-$40.00
Remaining Sets on page: $15.00-$25.00 per set

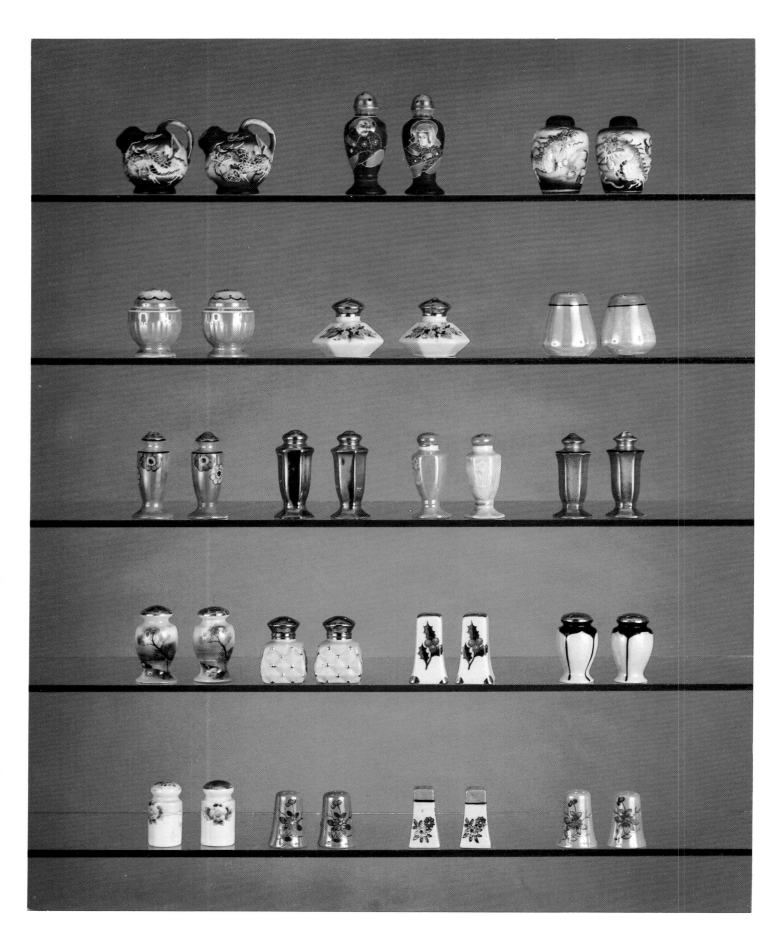

118

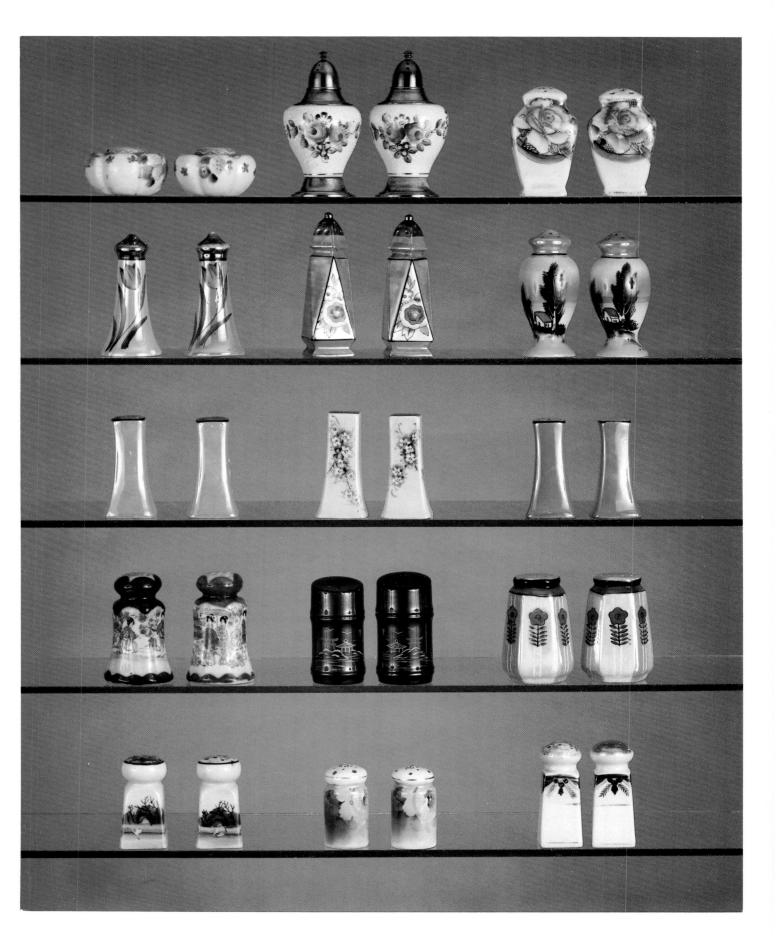

METAL

Mostly all of the black-and-white pot metal sets are decorated in a Pennsylvania Dutch design. Since Book One was published, much new information has become available on these attractive sets. My thanks, to Trish Claar for information about several companies that distributed the black-and-white sets. Two of the companies, both of New York, were Davis Products and Starke Design. There are records of John Wright and Wilton Products, which may possibly be the same company that operated out of Wrightsville, Pennsylvania. These companies were generally active between 1949 and 1960.

On the top shelf is the only miniature black-and-white set I have ever seen. I have no idea how many of these were made. The next set is the medium-sized washer. (There is also a larger size washer, which is not pictured.)

I found the rocking horses and the peacocks in the center row to be very charming sets, both nicely decorated. In the last row, there is an Amish man on his horse at one end, and a man with a wheelbarrow at the other. In the center are two interesting sets, although the man and lady *are* rather rough looking characters! In Helene Guarnaccia's second shaker book, in fact, this man has been arrested. I'm not sure which set is right, but you can be sure that they all sat on the same shelf in some store where people could just pick out what they felt was a pair. The clerks never knew the difference...nor did they care. This is undoubtedly where many mismatched sets have come from. The little old lady in the rocker is also very nice and quite desirable since she is not as easy to find as the Amish people in rockers.

With the exception of the last row, the shakers on the next page are a series of silver-colored metal shakers. I was helping a friend, Marge Shuty, move from her gift shop upon her retirement, and came across this series still packed in the original box. Only one set was missing! I thought that it was an exceptionally nice selection of animals, birds and water-related sets.

The dogs in the last row are silver-plated. The wonderful Scottie set in the center of this row has a chrome finish and is a great Art Deco set. The gavels are also of nice quality with a painted silver finish. With the exception of the silver-plated dogs, which are not marked, all of the sets on this page were made in Japan.

The last page is truly a mixture of metal sets. The first set appears to be hand-made. It is a glass shaker covered with a pierced casing which is marked "Sterling." The next set is silver-plated and is a souvenir of Washington, D. C. The last set in the row is aluminum. In the center of Row Two is a set given to me by my friend Mary as a joke. I think, however, that it is a very nice set! The lower half of the shaker is cobalt blue glass and the shakers rest on a molded leaf holder. The last two rows on this page consist of the metal tray sets, very easily found, yet fun to collect and popular with collectors as well.

With the exception of Row One, all the sets were made in Japan.

PAGE 121:
Row 1:	(1) $12.00-$15.00	(2) $15.00-$18.00	(3) $10.00-$12.00
Row 2:	All Sets $10.00-$12.00		
Row 3:	(1) $10.00-$12.00	(2) $12.00-$15.00	(3) $12.00-$15.00
Row 4:	(1) $10.00-$12.00	(2) $12.00-$15.00	(3) $10.00-$12.00
Row 5:	All Sets $15.00-$18.00		

PAGE 122:
Rows 1, 2, 3 & 4:	All Sets $8.00-$10.00		
Row 5: (1) $18.00-$20.00		(2) $25.00-$30.00	(3) $10.00-$12.00

PAGE 123:
Row 1:	(1) $25.00-$35.00	(2) $20.00-$25.00	(3) $15.00-$18.00
Row 2:	(1) $8.00-$10.00	(2) $12.00-$15.00	(3) $12.00-$15.00
Row 3:	(1) $8.00-$10.00	(2) $10.00-$12.00	(3) $6.00-$8.00
Rows 4 & 5:	All Sets: $5.00-$7.00		

121

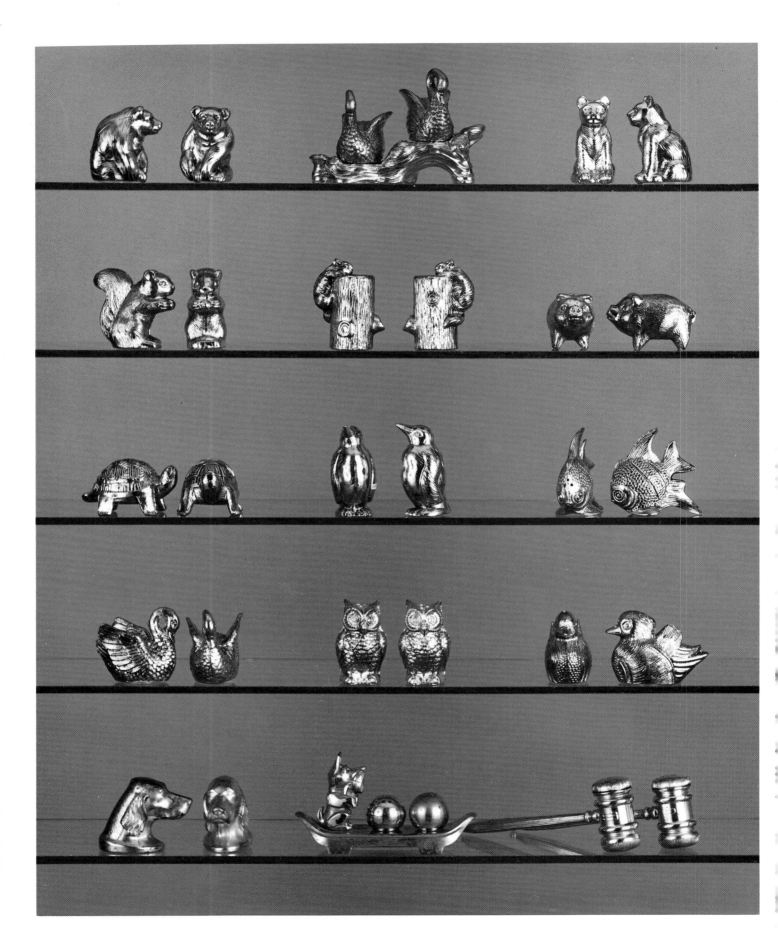

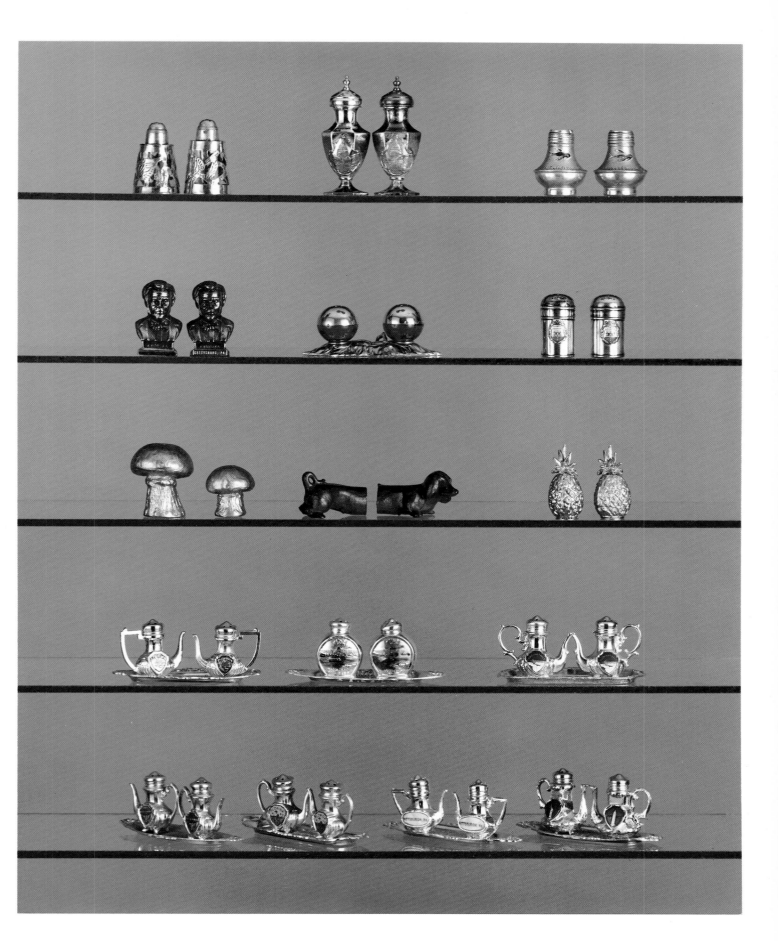

MINIATURES

In Book One I featured three pages of miniature shakers, all made by Arcadia Ceramics, from Arcadia, California. This time I have a mixture of all types of mini-sets.

In Row One, the first and last sets were used on airlines. They really should have been with the advertising sets; however, I was afraid they would become lost on the page! It is much easier to see the detail on them when they are pictured with shakers of the same size. The first airline is TWA; it flies out of Pittsburgh, so I do know it is still in business. The other set is from Northwest Airlines; I'm not so sure that one is still in business. Many of the smaller airlines keep disappearing. Those of you who thought to save these little shakers throughout the years will be surprised to watch the prices rise on them.

The second set in this row is a pair of monks. They were made in Hong Kong. This is the tiniest set I have ever seen. The bottom can be removed to fill them. They are made of plastic.

The thimble and thread is from Arcadia and exhibits a lot of gold trim. Other sets on the page that were made by Arcadia are: the chair and clock in the center of Row Two; the bathtub with kettle and the washtub with scrub board in Row Four; also the oyster and lobster at the end of Row Five.

The coal stove and bucket in Row Two, the pie a la mode in Row Three, and the crabs, first set in Row Five, are all marked "Japan." The other sets are unmarked; they are more than likely made in the USA, however, I do not believe Arcadia made any of these sets.

The second set in Row Three could also fit in the advertising section. It is a hot dog with a bottle of "Coke." The bottle is a very good replica of the real thing and the name can clearly be read. This set does merit a high price. The last set in this row is a bucket of paint with a paint brush. There is a decal on the front of the paint can that reads: "Hershey 50th Anniversary." Some people would also add this set to the advertising section. I just like to add Hershey to my snack list; in fact, I have a bag of Kisses beside me right now!

Row 1: (1) $6.00-$8.00   (2) $6.00-$8.00   (3) $15.00-$18.00   (4) $8.00-$10.00
Row 2: (1) $18.00-$20.00   (2) $35.00-$40.00   (3) $15.00-$18.00
Row 3: (1) $15.00-$18.00   (2) $20.00-$25.00   (3) $30.00-$35.00   (4) $15.00-$18.00
Row 4: (1) $35.00-$40.00   (2) $25.00-$30.00   (3) $25.00-$30.00
Row 5: (1) $20.00-$25.00   (2) $18.00-$20.00   (3) $35.00-$40.00

MINIATURES: UNDER THREE INCHES

I include these sets in the miniature category because they are all less than three inches in height. Many of the little china animal sets have been offered through the years, such as the giraffe and zebra sets in Row One, and the three sets in Row Two. The elephants in the center of Row One are ceramic.

The set of dressed raccoons at the end of Row Three are ceramic also, and the remaining sets on the page are china.

In Row Five, the first set is not marked; however, I do believe it was American-made. The last set in this row is Rosemeade. There is a page of Rosemeade shakers in the American-made section. It also includes some history about this popular company.

Unless otherwise mentioned, all the sets were made in Japan. They date from the 1940's to 1950's.

The Rosemeade Set at the end of Row Five is valued at: $35.00-$40.00
The remaining Sets are: $8.00-$12.00

127

MOTHER AND BABY AND PIGGY-BACKS

There are several different series of these wonderful sets, which are of course extremely collectible. The first and third set in Row One and the last set in Row Two are from the same series; they are hand-painted and colorful and seem to stand out among the rest of the shakers. Ceramic Arts Studio also did a series of mother-and-baby sets, some of which are included in the American-made section.

Just as in real life, these shaker children have a hard time staying on Mom's lap! In many instances, just walking past the shaker cabinet will cause the baby to fall. If you have had this problem, just place a rubber band (gumband, if you live in Pittsburgh...) around the mother and baby in order to hold the set securely. Cellophane tape is a poor solution because, in addition to leaving a sticky residue on the shaker, it can take much of the paint with it when it is removed. Rubber bands, therefore, work much better to hold any type of nester set intact.

The center set in Row One is a Japanese imitation of Elsie the Borden Cow and her twins (and, according to a late 1950's postcard from the Borden Company, she *did* have twins). Since this cow has no daisies around her neck, many collectors would not accept this set as representing Elsie and her twins, Latabee and Lobelia. (The names of the twins can be found in "Advertising Dolls" by Joleen Robinson and Kay Sellers...I really didn't make them up!) Whether or not one accepts this as an Elsie, therefore, is strictly up to the individual collector.

As you can see, the babies are held in many different positions: in arms, on backs, in laps and in pouches. This kind of variety adds a great deal of interest to any collection.

The last row consists of Piggy-Back sets. The shaker on the bottom has a flat surface on which the top shaker rests. Again, a rubber band will help to keep this set intact. Many people who have this type of shaker in their collections never knew that they were meant to be placed like this. I was one of these collectors, in fact, until I saw a piggy-back set in someone else's collection. I do not know how many other sets there are in this series. They are, however, a delight to own. The sets are all hand-painted and date from the late 1940's or early 1950's.

The mother-and-baby sets are all ceramic except for "Elsie" and the white bears in Row Three which are porcelain. All of these shakers were produced throughout the 1950's and were all made in Japan. All the shakers on this page, mother-and-baby or piggy-backs, are considered to be "Nesters."

Row 1: (1) $25.00-$30.00   (2) $35.00-$45.00   (3) $25.00-$30.00
Row 2: (1) $20.00-$25.00   (2) $15.00-$20.00   (3) $45.00-$50.00
Row 3: (1) $15.00-$18.00   (2) $18.00-$20.00   (3) $22.00-$28.00
Row 4: (1) $22.00-$28.00   (2) $22.00-$28.00   (3) $32.00-$38.00   (4) $22.00-$28.00

NESTERS

As most of us know, nesters are those sets in which one shaker rests entirely upon the other shaker in some way. Since there are so many different ones to collect, many people base their entire collections on this type of shaker. Although you will find a few others throughout the book in various categories, I wanted to show at least one full page to give you some idea of the variety one can find.

Contrary to what many collectors have thought, most of the sets on this page are American-made. The first two sets in Row One and the horse in Row Three are marked Japan; the last set in Row One is from Taiwan. All the remaining sets, I believe, were made in this country. Although many of them look like they may have been made by Parkcraft, they are unmarked and so one cannot be sure. For the first time however, there is a growing interest among collectors to discover who really made these shakers. Many old gift catalogs have been surfacing and are helping immensely in identifying shakers, especially the unmarked ones. Two of the sets pictured here are marked. The first set in Row Four (the small chicken on the basket) is impressed "Trevewood" and the fisherman in the boat in the center of Row Five has a paper label marked "Elbee Art, Cleveland, Ohio." The importance of these labels cannot be over estimated; without this label marked "Elbee Art," for example, this particular set would be totally unidentifiable. Well, we have two more company names to work with and, if you have others out there, please let us know!

The shakers on the top shelf are the most recent, made after 1970. All the others date from 1950 to 1960. All of these sets, incidentally, are made of ceramic. Many of them were sold by Heather House to members of their salt-and-pepper club. Other gift houses had shaker catalogs as well. Since I am always looking for any of these catalogs, please let me know if you have any available...photocopies are fine.

Row 1:	(1) $10.00-$12.00	(2) $8.00-$10.00	(3) $10.00-$12.00
Row 2:	(1) $12.00-$15.00	(2) $12.00-$15.00	(3) $8.00-$10.00
Row 3:	(1) $10.00-$12.00	(2) $12.00-$15.00	(3) $10.00-$12.00
Row 4:	(1) $8.00-$10.00	(2) $10.00-$12.00	(3) $10.00-$12.00	(4) $12.00-$15.00
Row 5:	(1) $10.00-$12.00	(2) $15.00-$18.00	(3) $10.00-$12.00	

NODDERS

Since the nodders rank high on the list of very desirable shakers, they have become extremely hard to find, and the most unusual sets are bringing outrageous prices. All of the sets pictured here have "Patent TT" impressed on the bottom. Five of the sets, however, are also stamped or have a paper label stating that they were made in Japan. I also have two sets (not pictured), one of which is impressed "Pat. TK" and stamped "Made in Occupied Japan" and the other is impressed "Pat. KS" and stamped "Japan" with a pre-war logo. My attempts to find information on these patent marks have so far been unsuccessful, but I nevertheless believe that these sets, even when not actually marked "Japan," were all made in that country. Since none of these nodders were offered through the shaker clubs or gift catalogs of the 1950's, and since the earlier Japanese marks have been found on several sets, it seems reasonable to assume that the majority of these sets were produced in Japan throughout the 1930's and 1940's.

All of the sets pictured are porcelain and hand-painted. The more easily found sets are those with the rose-decorated bases. The shakers in some of these are unusual enough, however, to make the entire set more desirable. An example of this is the Dutch couple on the top row; since the shakers depict people, this becomes a premium set, even though the base is the more common type. The sailboats in the center of Row Two are also unusual. Unusual or not, however, with the demand for nodders, they are all becoming increasingly hard to find.

Now we come to the "impossible-to-find" sets. These barely affordable sets are those with the figural bottoms, such as the second set in Row One. Next to this charming couple are a mother and baby kangaroo, both of which nod. The kangaroo set, although not nearly so hard to find as set two, is still scarce and very different from the common kangaroo sets, in which the baby just sits in the pouch and the mother is made all in one piece. The last set in this row is also worth a special mention. The nicely decorated round base and the colorful nodding Indians combine to create a most appealing set.

Row Five features two sets of nodding skulls! The first set is gray and rather morbid looking but the other set, in addition to having weird rhinestone eyes, has its lower row of teeth as part of the holder. When the head nods, it appears as though it is laughing at you--a bit strange, to say the least! Morbid and strange, notwithstanding, both sets are high on the desirable list. The bull and matador set in the center of this row is also a super set to find. It has a mustard pot in the middle of the base with a lid shaped like a hat. Since the bull and the matador are already nodding at each other, all you need to complete the scene is a red cape. (Maybe a red napkin will do...) This set is wonderfully decorated and merits the high price it commands.

A word about the construction of these sets is probably in order at this time. Each shaker has a small extension on each side of it, and the bottom part of the shaker fits into the base about 1½" to 2". There is a cork in the bottom of each shaker to hold the salt or pepper. The extensions on the sides of the shaker fit into notches in the base, allowing it to rock back and forth as it sits on the base and, when filled, the shakers "nod" even better. Be very careful when you buy nodders-always check both extensions on the shaker, because if one is chipped off, it will no longer rock. Since many people look for odd nodders and good bases to complete their sets, it is a good idea to save any parts from a set which is broken-you might be able to trade one piece for a *nodder* one!

Row 1: (1) $35.00-$40.00	(2) $275.00-300.00	(3) $85.00-$95.00	(4) $45.00-$55.00
Row 2: (1) $35.00-$40.00	(2) $45.00-$50.00	(3) $30.00-$35.00	
Row 3: (1) $35.00-$40.00	(2) $30.00-$35.00	(3) $30.00-$35.00	
Row 4: (1) $45.00-$50.00	(2) $30.00-$35.00	(3) $30.00-$35.00	(4) $30.00-$35.00
Row 5: (1) $65.00-$75.00	(2) $85.00-$95.00	(3) $45.00-$55.00	

NOVELTY: MISCELLANEOUS

The next three "catch-all" pages are made up of sets that didn't seem to fit into any of the other sections or seemed to pop up at the very last minute.

The vegetable-and-fruit people are very popular with collectors. The first set in Row Two is dated 1956 and is signed NAPCO, which is the trademark of the National Potteries Corporation of Bedford, Ohio. This company, which is still in business, began in 1938 and not only imports and distributes their wares, but also manufactures some of the items they have on the market. NAPCO is responsible for many of the shakers which are found in a series. The set pictured here is a good example of the originality of NAPCO'S work and there is an entire series of shakers like this which feature various sports. Our thanks to NAPCO for caring enough to sign and date most of their pieces – it certainly is a boon to the collector!

The cow set in the center of Row Four is another set which is positively identified for it too is signed, in this instance, by Holt-Howard and dated 1958. The Holt-Howard Company, which was located in Stamford, Connecticut, also did some manufacturing as well as importing. This set is really amusing; when you shake these cows, their tongues pop out! Holt-Howard has done many of the novelty shakers we all look for...so our thanks to them also for helping us by dating and signing their sets.

The corn people have no mark, but they have that "American Look." The cute eggs at the end of Row Three are bisque and one of the later sets on this page. The watermelon people in the center of Row Two are truly adorable as well as being quite unusual...this is the first watermelon set I have seen in "people" form.

The fork and spoon in the very center of the page is the oldest set dating from the 1940's while the "eggheads" are the youngest and date from the late 1970's. The majority of the remaining sets are from the 1950's. Unless otherwise indicated, the sets were made in Japan.

From the impish bumblebees in Row Five to the spooky ghosts in Row Three to the coquettish ladybugs which end the page, this selection really deserves the designation of Figural Novelty Shakers.

Row 1: (1) $20.00-$25.00	(2) $35.00-$40.00	(3) $65.00-$75.00
Row 2: (1) $40.00-$50.00	(2) $18.00-$22.00	(3) $30.00-$35.00
Row 3: (1) $15.00-$18.00	(2) $15.00-$18.00	(3) $10.00-$12.00
Row 4: (1) $25.00-$30.00	(2) $15.00-$18.00	(3) $25.00-$30.00
Row 5: (1) $12.00-$15.00	(2) $18.00-$20.00	(3) $10.00-$12.00

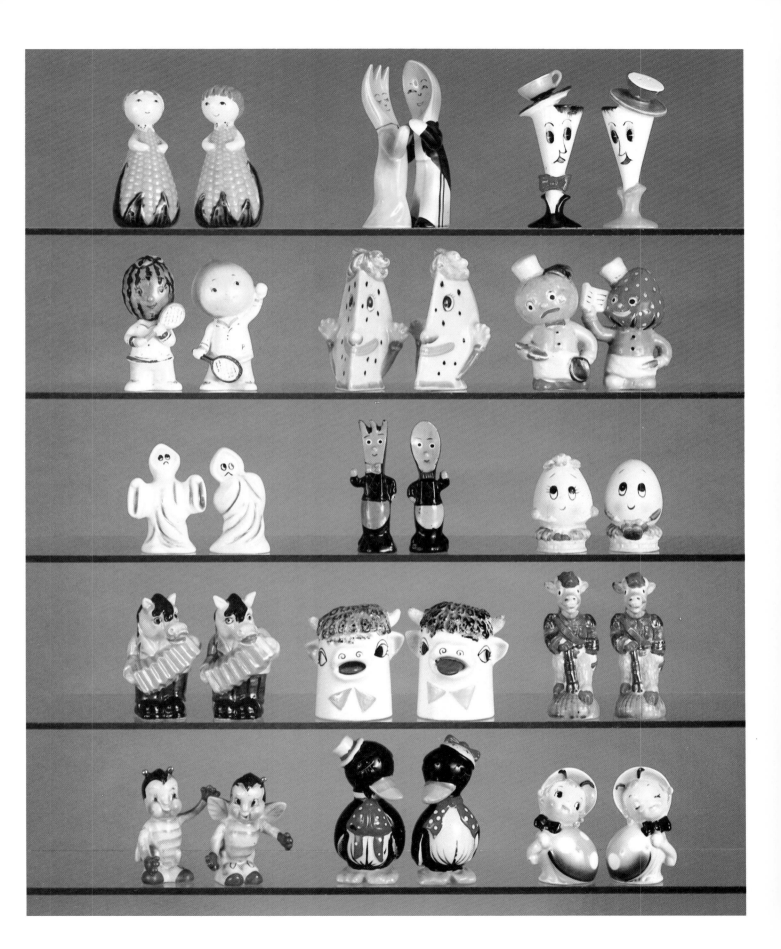

NOVELTY: MISCELLANEOUS (continued)

The following pages exhibit sets of novelty shakers that did not fit into any particular group; therefore, they all fit into the world of the miscellaneous. This will at least give collectors an idea of the diversity in the shaker world.

In Row One, the first set is a wonderful pair of Oriental type sandals. They are made of porcelain and are very nicely hand-painted. The next set of undergarments would add a unique touch to a table setting for a bachelor party! The next set of shoes resting on a shoe rack is a much sought-after set. I am sure many people have just the shoes, not even knowing the rack exists.

The first two sets in Row Two are "aching feet." Rumor has it that they were designed by a person who had just returned from a day at Disneyland!! The next set are happy feet--they stayed home!

The first and last sets in the center row are the same geometric design; however, the decorations are different. The hand-painted coffee grinders in the center of the row have a charm of their own.

The first set in Row Four is obviously a souvenir of Indianapolis, Indiana, considering that they are signed as such. The last two sets in this row speak for themselves. All three sets are light-weight ceramic.

The sets in the shapes if "S" and "P" have a story behind them. The shakers were manufactured by Camark Pottery of Camden, Arkansas. The pottery opened in 1926 and was reportedly sold in 1966. This set was made in the early 1950's for use as a promotional gimmick for employees of different companies. A card was given with each set that read: "P is for Pepper, S is for Salt: P is for Profits, S is for Sales: P. S. They Do the Job." I would imagine after reading the card, if you would use the shakers in your home, it would be a constant reminder to do better, especially if they sit on the breakfast table every day! The sets come in many different colors as well as with the lustre finish.

The second set in Row Five are books "Peppery Tales" and "Salty Stories." They are signed: c. CC Co. I have no information on this one; however, I am sure they were American-made. The broken heart with the gold arrow through it is unmarked, and again, I believe it is American-made.

With the exception of the last row which are all American-made, all of the sets were made in Japan in the late 1940's to 1950's.

Row 1: (1) $10.00-$12.00   (2) $10.00-$12.00   (3) $15.00-$18.00
Row 2: All Sets: $8.00-$10.00
Row 3: All Sets: $8.00-$10.00
Row 4: All Sets: $8.00-$10.00
Row 5: All Sets: $10.00-$12.00

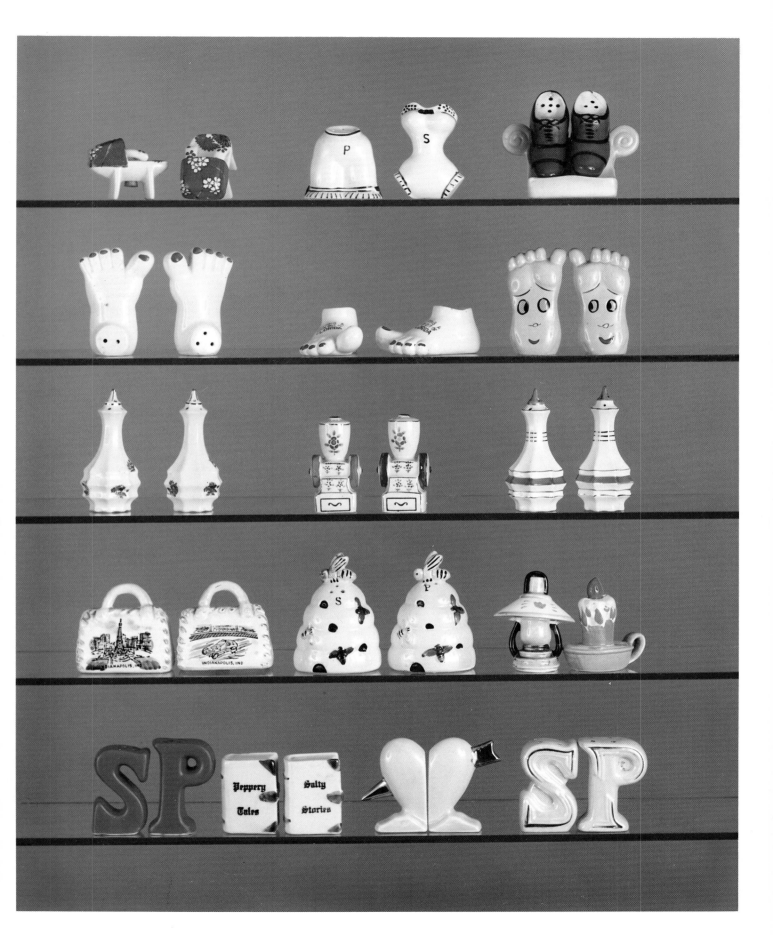

NOVELTY: MISCELLANEOUS (continued)

The first and third set, in the top row, are very nice replicas of old steins. They would surely add a little spice to a stein collection.

The center set is Row One was made by Bill's Specialty Mfg. Co. If you recall, they also did many of the mini-beer bottle shakers. You will find this heavy porcelain shaker with many variations in designs. Many souvenir sets were made also. Most of the sets were trimmed in 22-karat gold.

The first two sets in Row Two are also made of porcelain. The center set is very popular and comes in all types of decoration. The shakers lift out of the top of the binoculars. The last set in the row is a souvenir from the Golden Nugget Casino, though this may be the only thing they came home with!

I have had the first and last sets, in Row Three for a long time. I cannot find any information concerning the mark on them. I am sure they were made in the USA, but they remain a puzzle. The mark is a hand-painted blue "N" with a different number for each set. The shakers are made of a heavy ceramic, yet they are delicately hand-painted. I would welcome any information on this mark.

In the center of Row Four is a charming red barn and silo. The shakers fit snugly together. They are made of light-weight ceramic and date from the 1970's.

The last row consists of a sprinkling of the civil war type shakers to be found. The first set of Confederate hats and the cannons all feature a decal of the Confederate flag, as does the last hat in the row, paired with a Union forces hat.

Unless mentioned above, all sets were made in Japan in 1945 to 1950 with the exception of the barn c. 1970's.

Row 1:	(1) $5.00-$7.00	(2) $8.00-$10.00	(3) $8.00-$10.00
Row 2:	(1) $8.00-10.00	(2) $15.00-$20.00	(3) $5.00-$7.00
Row 3:	(1) $8.00-10.00	(2) $8.00-10.00	(3) $5.00-$7.00
Row 4:	(1) $8.00-$10.00	(2) $8.00-$10.00	(3) $4.00-$6.00
Row 5:	(1) $8.00-$10.00	(2) $8.00-$10.00	(3) $10.00-$12.00

OCCUPIED JAPAN

Many people base their entire collections on shakers made in "Occupied Japan." Although the search for these shakers has not decreased at all, I must say the prices seem to have leveled out. There has not been much rise in prices since the first book. However, I assure you that the demand for them is still great and the less common sets do merit a high price.

Being a "period" collectible makes them very easy to date. All items exported from Japan from the end of World War II in 1945 until the peace treaty was signed April 28, 1952, had to be marked "Made in Occupied Japan." One can find the exact same sets, one marked "Occupied" while the other is just marked "Japan." This is a result of sets being made before the war and not shipped before the new law came into existence; the sets then had to be re-stamped "Occupied." This is the reason you will find several marks on shakers.

The set MUST be marked "Occupied Japan" or it cannot be included in this catagory, do not let anyone convince you otherwise.

In the center of the top shelf is one of the greatest sets I have seen in "Occupied" Japan. It is a chef standing at a stove; the top half of the chef lifts to find a mustard holder, and the two pots are the shakers. This set belongs to Betsy Zalewski, who has supplied me with several interesting sets throughout the book.

The set in the center of Row Three is also a fantastic set. It was given to me by my friend Mary, who edits what I write, before it gets to the editors from Collector Books!! I have a language of my own, which she aptly transforms into English! Getting back to the shakers, this little boy and girl are made of porcelain and have wonderful hand-painted features.

In the center of the bottom row is another unusual set. The duck on the basket in the center of the tray is a mustard holder, while the other two ducks are the shakers.

The frogs at the end of Row Five may not be a set. If I find that it is not, I will show the right set in the next book! The remaining sets on the page are fairly common.

	(1)	(2)	(3)
Row 1:	$12.00-$15.00	$65.00-$70.00	$12.00-$15.00
Row 2:	$12.00-$15.00	$15.00-$18.00	$12.00-$15.00
Row 3:	$12.00-$15.00	$50.00-55.00	$12.00-$15.00
Row 4:	$15.00-$18.00	$25.00-30.00	$15.00-$18.00
Row 5:	$15.00-$18.00	$30.00-$35.00	$15.00-$18.00

OCCUPIED JAPAN: (continued)

In the center of Row One is a very nice set of decaled shakers. The teapots on each end of this row are nicely hand-painted. The second set in Row Two is an extremely nice bisque set of birds perched in a holder. Their pastel shades make them very appealing.

All the sets in Rows Two and Four include trays or holders. Quite often the holders are the only part marked "Made in Occupied Japan." If you only have the shakers and they are not marked "Occupied," you are out of luck.

In the bottom row, on each end are two very large sets of shakers. They are brightly hand-painted, but greatly out of proportion to the other sets. I guess they fall into the category of range size sets. The beehive set in the center of this row belongs on a tray which I did not have; however, all the pieces are marked "Occupied."

There are hundreds of Occupied Japan sets to find; once you have collected all the common sets, the unique sets are a real challenge to find. I previously mentioned that the prices have leveled out in the past few years, but this will be temporary, I can assure you. The prices will rise again when the supply begins to dry up. So, buy what you can find now; you may not get a second chance.

Row 1: (1) $10.00-$12.00   (2) $12.00-$15.00   (3) $10.00-$12.00
Row 2: (1) $15.00-$18.00   (2) $25.00-$30.00   (3) $10.00-$12.00   (4) $15.00-$18.00
Row 3: (1) $12.00-$15.00   (2) $12.00-$15.00   (3) $12.00-$15.00   (4) $22.00-$25.00
Row 4: All Sets $15.00-$18.00
Row 5: (1) $20.00-$25.00   (2) $40.00-$45.00   (3) $20.00-$25.00

ONE-PIECE SHAKERS

If you would add the selection of one-piece shakers from this book to the sets in the first book, it would make a truly great collection. Although I have tried over the years to hold on to them, I always seem to find a collector friend with a sad expression and an even sadder story to match and I always end by giving them up!

I borrowed several sets from my English buddy Nigel Dalley; all of the sets on the top shelf and the bellhops on the second shelf are from his collection.

Most of the sets on the first two shelves are made of china and the first three sets are ingeniously hand-painted. The oriental girl, who is one of my all-time favorites, wears and apron which has a beaded effect and she is as delicate as she looks. I have been told that the last bellhop is rather new-an assertion about which I have my doubts. Since he does have old cork stoppers and his paint is of an earlier type, I feel he is at least from the 1960's at the latest. Although it is possible that this is a very fine reproduction of an older set, the newer sets just seem to lack the quality of the originals and this set does have the quality associated with the older sets.

The last three shelves feature wonderful one-piece "Longfellows." I think that the lion and the alligator are unique, but again, these are sets which just seem to slip through my little fingers! The poodle and the cow have the same early Japanese mark. Although the poodle is a very nice shaker, I would rather not comment on the pig and the cow!

With the exception of the lion and the alligator which are not marked, all of the shakers are marked "Japan." The first four sets are from the 1940's and the remaining ones are from the 1950-1960 period. The black cat is made of red clay and the rest of the shakers in the last three rows are ceramic.

Row 1: All sets $22.00-$25.00
Row 2: (1) $22.00-$25.00   (2) $20.00-$23.00   (3) $20.00-$23.00   (4) $22.00-$25.00
Row 3: Both Sets: $25.00-$30.00 each
Row 4: (1) $10.00-$12.00   (2) $25.00-$30.00
Row 5: Both Sets: $18.00-$22.00

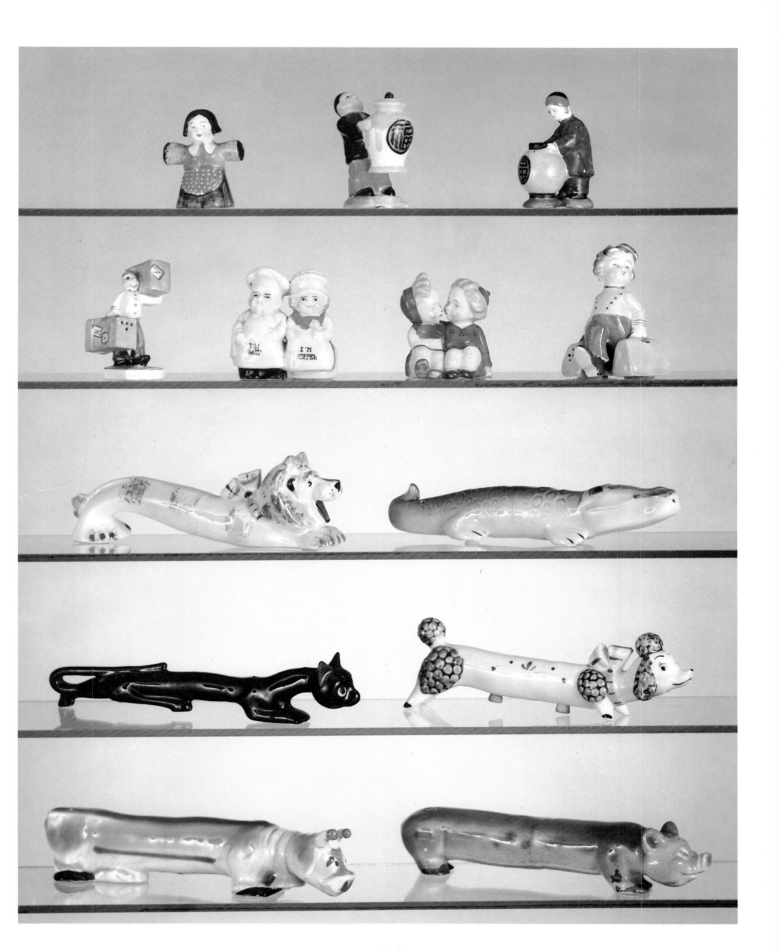

ONE-PIECE SHAKERS: (continued)

All of the one-piece shakers are interesting in different ways. Although the selection on this page may not appear as exciting as those on the first page, there are quite a few unusual sets here. Those on the top shelf are rather streamlined with an Art Deco flavor and the last set in this row is German with a lustre finish.

The first set in Row Two is an early set of hand-painted ducks from Japan; the second set, which is all white, shows two Spanish men sleeping (as was the person who was in charge of painting them)! The last set is a super 1950's set, very delicate with a flamingo and a palm tree attaches at the base – a terrific find for a flamingo collector.

The last set in the center row was also extremely delicate – my set, which was okay to photograph, was nevertheless broken in several places and it made the circular file shortly after the photography session ended.

The plastic clothespin works exactly like those we use on our generic dryers; it has the same spring action but is a bit more Art Deco-looking. Now the train has a story...it was formerly the "Loco from Ohio" which had a short layover in Pittsburgh. It is now the "Maryland Express." Needless to say, this was another set I really planned to keep, but it too went chugging down the track! I had never seen another shaker like it. I really had to pick it up and check it over several times before I could believe that it was really a shaker- and a really super one at that!

The last row is the "Strange but True" section! The first is a very unusual one-piece shaker, since it is not common to find this type made of wood. The second is shaped like an egg timer, with salt filling the bottom and pepper the top. Made of glass, wood and metal, each end slides open to use the condiments. The third set in this row is lucite and the fourth is a mechanical robot-how modern can we get? If you wind up the robot, he will walk to the other end of the table and personally deliver the salt and pepper...what more can I Say?

The ducks which are c. 1940 are the earliest set and the robot is the latest, made in the late 1970's. The rest date somewhere in between. The clothespin was made in Hong Kong, the robot in Taiwan, the last set in Row One in Germany, and the remaining sets were made in Japan.

Row 1:	(1) $8.00-$10.00	(2) $8.00-$10.00	(3) $8.00-$10.00	(4) $12.00-$15.00
Row 2:	(1) $12.00-$15.00	(2) $10.00-$12.00	(3) $22.00-$25.00	
Row 3:	(1) $10.00-$12.00	(2) $8.00-$10.00	(3) $12.00-$15.00	
Row 4:	(1) $8.00-$10.00	(2) $22.00-$25.00		
Row 5:	(1) $3.00-$5.00	(2) $10.00-$12.00	(3) $10.00-$12.00	(4) $12.00-$15.00

PLASTIC PLUS

The next three pages are a "catch all" for sets we all have, but do not know how to classify. Well, neither do I! That is why I placed them here.

The first page consists of rather normal, popular plastic sets. The first set with the cupid is unusual. The second set in this row has strange looking peanuts hanging from a very delicate plastic tree. There are several little birds attached to the branches.

The next three rows contain shakers that are very popular today. The piano is one of several varieties. When you push the keys, the shakers pop out of the top. The notes on the next set are the shakers. They will hold about all the spices one should use in a day! The guitar at the end of this row is one-piece and sits on a rack.

In Row Three the first and last shakers combine to make a delightful set of wind-up shakers. The butler and maid will deliver your spices right to your plate, (if aimed correctly that is.) The bowling pins in the center set are shakers and the ball open to use as a mustard or sugar.

The bottom row consists of a pump and bucket set, in which you can push the pump handle and the shakers will rise on top, while the bucket serves as a mustard or sugar. Next is an oyster shell with two pearl-shaped shakers inside. Last is a variation of the plastic toasters. The cupid set in Row One and the butler and maid set in Row Three were made in Hong Kong; the remaining sets are American-made, c. 1950's.

The shakers on the next page are all combinations of metal holders with glass or plastic shakers. The only plastic shakers on the page are the weights on the scale and the candles in the holders in Row Three. All the other shakers are glass and all the holders are metal. There are very similar sets where the entire set is plastic. The center set in Row Three has a little flower post in the middle which is for toothpicks. The painter's palette in the center of Row Four also has a small holder for toothpicks. It is also a very nice set to own.

The last page of this group has quite a variety of shakers. The first set in Row One sits on a lucite holder; the shakers are metal. This is a very popular Art Deco-type set and comes in a variety of styles. The plastic clocks are nicely molded with great detail. The last set in this row is a variation of the umbrella sets; the holder is metal.

The first set in the bottom row is very old. It comes with a little spoon for the gondola, which is a salt holder, the shaker is for pepper. The next set is a very delicate pair of pocket watches. They rest quite nicely on the rack provided with the set. The stem of the watch comes out in order to fill the shaker. They are all plastic. The base and the shakers in the third set are glass. The top part of the holder is plastic. The final sets are just two of the many lantern style sets to be found. They are very nice sets; the base is usually glass and the shades are plastic.

This assortment was produced, mainly, in the 1940's to 1950's era. All are American-made.

PAGE 149:
Row 1: All Sets: $5.00-$7.00
Row 2: All Sets: $12.00-$15.00 set
Row 3: (1) $22.00-$25.00 set   (2) $10.00-$12.00   (3) $22.00-$25.00 set
Row 4: (1) $18.00-$20.00   (2) $15.00-$18.00   (3) $10.00-$12.00

PAGE 150:
All Sets on Page: $8.00-10.00 per set

PAGE 151:
Row 1: (1) $30.00-$35.00   (2) $5.00-$7.00   (3) $8.00-$10.00
Row 2: All Sets: $7.00-$10.00
Row 3: (1) $6.00-$8.00   (2) $10.00-$12.00   (3) $6.00-$8.00
Row 4: (1) $8.00-$10.00   (2) $10.00-$12.00   (3) $10.00-$12.00   (4&5) $5.00-$7.00

SHAKERS PLUS

This is a rather a "catch-all" section for shakers that come with, or are attached to something other than salt-and-peppers. I have seen a recent increase in people searching for this type of set, yet others do not even know such sets exist. I must say that most of these sets would fit into a strange-but-true section.

Row One consists of the shakers with vinegar-and-oil containers. The shakers on sets one and three have corks at the base that fit snugly into the vinegar-and-oil containers. Therefore, every time you would use the shakers, you would also have to shake the vinegar and oil! I wonder how long it would take for the corks to grow weary from all the pressure and shower your food with some unexpected spices! The shakers on the center set just rest on top of the vinegar and oil containers and need only to be lifted off to be used.

In the second row, we have salt-and-pepper, egg-cup combos! In sets one and three, the shakers are the little egg-shaped heads on the people. The bases are used to hold your "real" soft boiled egg as you eat it. However, that's not all folks! If you wish to take your egg out of the shell and chop it up with butter and salt and pepper, of course one can invert the base of the third set and have a larger bowl to accommodate your needs. The center set, in this row, also has the larger bowls. It also has a rim around the base to hold discarded egg shells on your spoon. The shakers on this set are the hats. By the way, you can just keep the shakers in your pocket until you are finished with your egg!

The sets on each end of Row Three consist of a normal set of shakers; in this case, they are both chickens. The larger chicken in the group was, prior to the 1950's, a grease holder. People use to save bacon drippings or other meat fats to use for frying eggs or potatoes or whatever.

People no longer do that, so these "grease" containers are now used as sugar bowls. Next we will use them to hold the pills that take the place of all the things you previously used them for!

The center set in Row Three is titled, "Spoon Nest." Now, the two little chicks resting on top of the holder, are the shakers. You can see in the photo around the top rim where the chicks are sitting; there are little notches to hold your spoons! I have just one last suggestion for uses of this set. One could invert this base and use the large inner portion to stuff any new ideas for more shakers of this type!

The last set in Row Three is porcelain and is unmarked. The remaining sets on the page were made in Japan. Circa 1940-1950's.

Row 1:	(1) $30.00-$35.00	(2) $45.00-$50.00	(3) $30.00-$35.00
Row 2:	(1) $12.00-$15.00	(2) $18.00-$20.00	(3) $15.00-$18.00
Row 3:	(1) $20.00-$25.00	(2) $12.00-$15.00	(3) $20.00-$25.00

SPOON NEST

153

SHAKERS PLUS: (continued)

The top section of all the sets on this page are shakers. The bases on all the sets are sugar and creamers! Isn't that SPECIAL? This idea was good to help consolidate items on the dinner table. However, did anyone think about the corks falling out and spilling the spices into the sugar bowl?? I say this because I have experienced the taste of salt and sugar mixed! When I was a darling little child, I once filled the sugar bowl with salt as an April fool's joke! The way it turned out, the joke was on me. My mother wanted to wash the sugar bowl, so she poured the salt back into the sugar canister. It did not take long to discover the salt! I confessed to my little prank and as a reminder not to EVER do it again, I spent several weeks using up the mixed creation! That, however, was not the worst of my punishment. My brothers and sisters also had to help me use up the mixture. My shins took a long time to heal from all of them kicking me under the breakfast table! Did you ever eat rolled oats with salty-sugar?

The sets in Row One are unusual, because the ones you most often find in this style are chickens. The first set is bears; it is also the newest on the page. The second set is large poodles; they have a red clay base, as does the first set of chickens in Row Three. The last set in Row One is parrots. The paint is not very good on this set.

The last set in Row Two is a heavy porcelain. Unless mentioned, all the remaining sets are ceramic. Chickens are very popular to collect, so I am sure many people would enjoy adding this selection to their collection. We never use our shakers anyway, so you would not have to worry about the corks coming out!

I must warn you, these are very large sets. They would be great for the window sills. All of the sets were made in Japan. The last sets in both Rows One and Three were distributed by Relco. Sets span the 1940's-1950's.

All Sets on Page: $15.00-$20.00 per set

154

SIGHTSEEING

The first two sets pictured on this page are from the 1939 World's Fair. "The World of Tomorrow" was the theme and the Trylon and Perisphere the symbol. Ironically, due to the onset of the war in Europe, many of the fair's activities were curtailed in 1940. The first set is made of plastic and was manufactured by the Emeloid Company of Arlington, New Jersey. It is one-piece and comes in several color combinations. The second set is silver-plate made by Wm. Rodgers. It is a wonderful set that I acquired from my mother's collection. The shakers are glass. The third set in Row One is from the 1964 World's Fair. Its theme was "Peace through Understanding" and its symbol a 250 ton stainless steel globe. This set of shakers, however, is much lighter! The shakers, as well as the tray, were made in Japan.

Wonderful places to visit are represented on the second shelf. The first is from the Grand Canyon National Park, Arizona; one of the most colorful, awesome, natural wonders of the world. The second set pictures Mount Rushmore National Memorial in the Black Hills of South Dakota. It was designed by an American artist, Gutzon Borglum, who supervised the work on his marvelous granite carving until his death in 1941. The sixty-foot heads of George Washington, Thomas Jefferson, Theodore Roosevelt and Abraham Lincoln were unveiled one at a time from 1930 until 1939. Several much nicer figural shaker sets can be found of this memorial.

The third set in Row Two as well as the two sets in Row Four are from Niagara Falls. It is estimated that the falls were formed about 12,000 years ago. (I'm sure that they were named much later!) The scenes most often found on these souvenir shakers are the Canadian Horseshoe Falls or the American Falls. Goat Island in the Niagara River divides the two sides. A treaty between Canada and the United States requires that the flow of water over the falls be regulated. The Canadian side drops about 176 feet and carries 90% of the water, while the American side drops about 193 feet and carries 10%. The Canadian Falls, which is substantially larger, is shaped like a horseshoe-thus its name. The American side is basically straight. It is a super place to visit and the surrounding towns are full of museums and great sights. Two of the sets pictured here feature the "Maid of the Mist," the boat that takes you under the falls-if you dare! The set in Row Two fits together, joining the American and Canadian sides together. The set in the center of Row Four is an interesting one; the boat is a shaker as well as the removable side of the falls! The other set on this shelf is merely a blank cylinder-type shaker with a decal – in this case, one of Niagara Falls.

The Mackinac Bridge in the center of the page is the only bridge shaker set that I have ever seen. Thanks to the generosity of my friend Tee in Cincinnati, I was able to use it for this book. The actual bridge is five miles long and spans the Straits of Mackinac, connecting the upper and lower peninsulas of Michigan. It runs from St. Ignace to Mackinaw City and although construction began in 1954, it was opened as a toll bridge in 1957. Now that the geography lesson is over, we can all begin to search for other shakers like this!

The first set in Row Five is a very old (c. 1930) glass set from England which has a very nicely done decal scene. On the other end of this row is a set from Disneyland; again decaled and rather common.

The center set was made in 1980 by Zoeller in Washington State. It is a replica of Mount St. Helen before and after the eruption on May 18, 1980. The top piece of the set cleverly fits back to make the mountain "whole" again. In addition, it states on the bottom of the shaker that it was made with ash from the actual eruption but it has a food-safe glaze. All the wonderful information that the collector needs is impressed on the bottom of this set. A hearty thanks to the manufacturer from the hundreds of collectors of the future! This set comes to you by way of the collection of Betsy Zalewski, another generous friend.

Unless noted otherwise, all the sets were made in Japan and are ceramic.

Row 1:	(1) $25.00-$30.00	(2) $35.00-$40.00	(3) $15.00-$18.00
Row 2:	(1) $12.00-$15.00	(2) $10.00-$12.00	(3) $18.00-$20.00
Row 3:	(1) $25.00-$30.00		
Row 4:	(1) $12.00-$15.00 set	(2) $25.00-$30.00	(3) $12.00-$15.00 set
Row 5:	(1) $10.00-$12.00	(2) $35.00-$40.00	(3) $8.00-$10.00

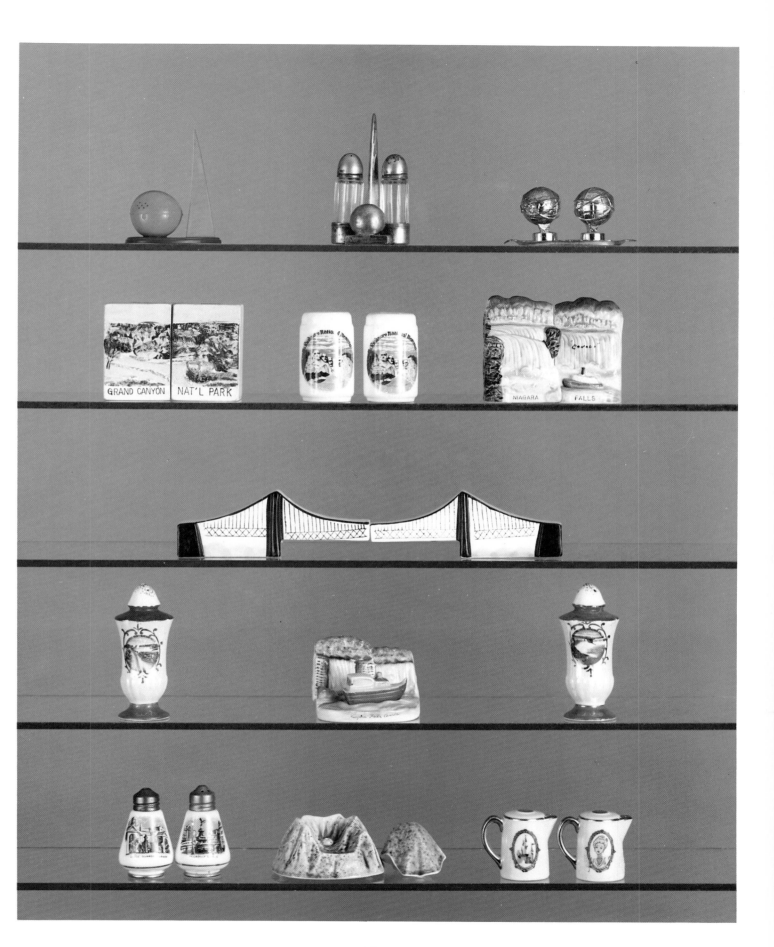

157

TRANSPORTATION

Modes of transportation are always fun to collect. The center set in Row One is the same size as the one in my first book; this one, however, is painted better and has more detail. The black trains in Row One and the cars in the center of Row Four are from the same series of shakers and are made in Japan. The large train, Row One; the white-and-gold sailboats at the end of Row Three and the trolleys in Row Four were also made in Japan. The other sets are unmarked and may be American-made.

The first and third sets in Row Two are metal and the red boat in the center is made of plastic with glass shakers. There has been quite an increase in the collecting of plastic shakers from the 1950's especially since they were mostly made in America. With the exception of the shakers in this row, all the sets are ceramic.

Many interesting specialized collections have been built around transportation sets. The first set in Row Four, for example, has "Desire" embossed on each end, possibly commemorating the famous play "A Streetcar Named Desire." Myriads of other sets are available, including cars, trucks, bicycles, etc. The field is virtually unlimited and the entire collection will take up a lot less room than even one Rolls Royce!

Row 1:	(1) $8.00-$10.00 set	(2) $30.00-$35.00	(3) $8.00-$10.00 set
Row 2:	(1) $10.00-$12.00	(2) $10.00-$12.00	(3) $8.00-$10.00
Row 3:	(1) $6.00-$8.00	(2) $8.00-$10.00	(3) $4.00-$6.00
Row 4:	All Sets: $8.00-$10.00		
Row 5:	All Sets: $8.00-$10.00		

159

WATER RELATED: FROGS

As I promised you in Book One, I am presenting my full page of frogs. For some reason, frogs are highly collectible – possibly because people are waiting for one to turn into a prince! (Or maybe think that frogs will keep you from "croaking.") In any event, frogs do make an unusual water-related collection, although one may soon exhaust the possibilities. Sylvia Tompkins, who has been voted the most avid collector of water-related sets in the Salt and Pepper Club, began running low on frogs, fish turtles and the like and began to add water hydrants, wells, water pumps, etc. So if you find a really strange aquatic item (in shaker from ONLY!), send it to Sylvia!

Before I find myself in deep water; however, I'd better introduce some of these frog sets to you. The center set on the top shelf was made for Sears, Roebuck & Company and is dated 1977. In the center of Row Four is a multi-piece set, consisting of a salt, a pepper and a mustard container, all contained on a tray. If you want to dive into collecting water-related shakers, this is a good place to begin.

The sets on the first page were all made in Japan, except for the first set in Row Four which is unmarked. They date from the 1940's until the late 1970's.

The next page contains a variety of water-related sets. This will give you a general idea of what can be included in a specialized collection of this type. Row One consists of lobsters. (Although they are all red, they are in no way connected with those served at the Red Lobster Restaurants!) The set in the center is my favorite. While photographing the shakers for this book, we took a ten minute break just waiting for the claws (which are on tiny springs) to stop waving so we could get on with it.

In addition to the lobsters, one can find seahorses, alligators, crocodiles, hippos, snails and turtles on this page. It is hard to imagine that even Sylvia could have run out of them. The very last set of turtles on this page is not marked; all the remaining sets were made in Japan, and again, they date from the 1940's until the last ten years or so.

Let's move on to the last page now and put the FIN-ishing touches on this section. Imagine a full wall covered with a glassed-in cabinet just deep enough to display one row of shakers per shelf, completely filled with every variety of fish shakers one could find. Think how wonderful this would look on the wall of a fishing lodge! No...I have never seen one either, but I bet it WOULD be nice.

With the exception of the second set in Row Three, which is not marked, all the sets are from Japan. I know I said this before, but some things need to be repeated...one could really get HOOKED on this section!

PAGE 161:
Row 1:	All Sets: $10.00-$12.00		
Row 2:	(1) $5.00-$7.00	(2) $12.00-$15.00	(3) $6.00-$8.00	(4) $8.00-$10.00
Row 3:	(1) $12.00-$15.00	(2) $5.00-$7.00	(3) $6.00-$8.00	(4) $8.00-$10.00
Row 4:	(1) $7.00-$9.00	(2) $35.00-$45.00	(3) $7.00-$9.00	
Row 5:	All Sets: $10.00-$12.00		

PAGE 162:
Row 1:	(1) $8.00-$10.00	(2) $22.00-$25.00	(3) $8.00-$10.00
Row 2:	(1) $10.00-$12.00	(2) $10.00-$12.00	(3) $12.00-$15.00
Row 3:	(1) $7.00-$9.00	(2) $7.00-$9.00	(3) $8.00-$10.00
Row 4:	All Sets: $7.00-$9.00		
Row 5:	All Sets: $10.00-$12.00		

PAGE 163;
Row 1:	(1) $6.00-$8.00	(2) $12.00-$15.00	(3) $6.00-$8.00	
Row 2:	(1) $12.00-$15.00	(2) $8.00-$10.00	(3) $6.00-$8.00	(4) $12.00-15.00
Row 3:	(1) $6.00-$8.00	(2) $6.00-$8.00	(3) $8.00-$10.00	(4) $8.00-10.00
Row 4:	(1) $12.00-$15.00	(2) $15.00-$18.00	(3) $12.00-$15.00	
Row 5:	(1) $12.00-$15.00	(2) $15.00-$18.00	(3) $15.00-$18.00	

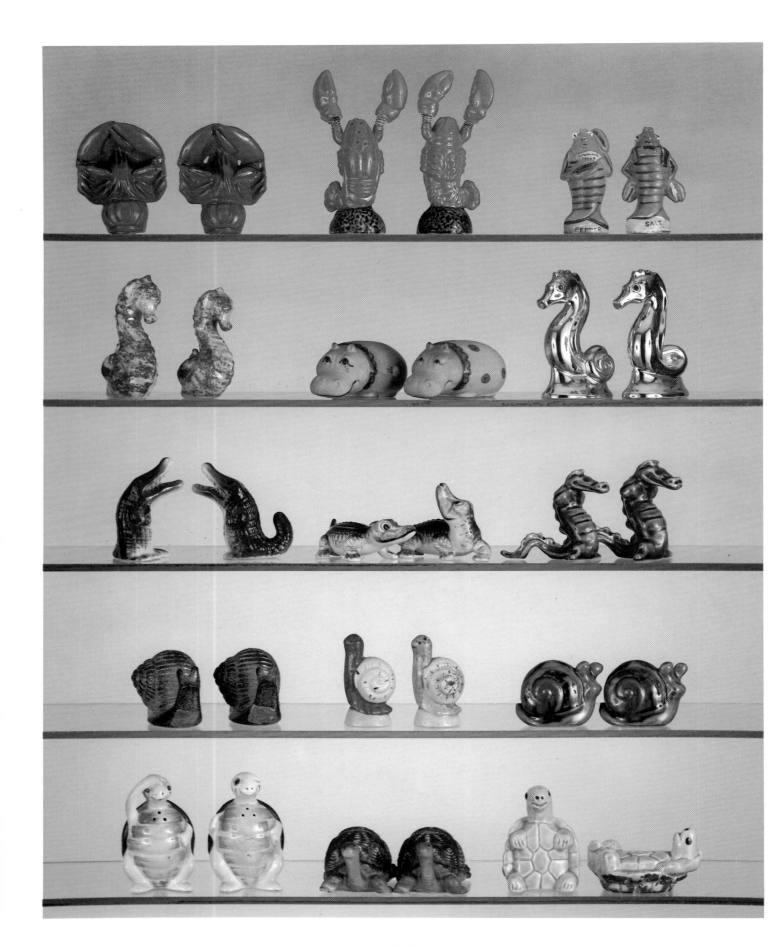

162

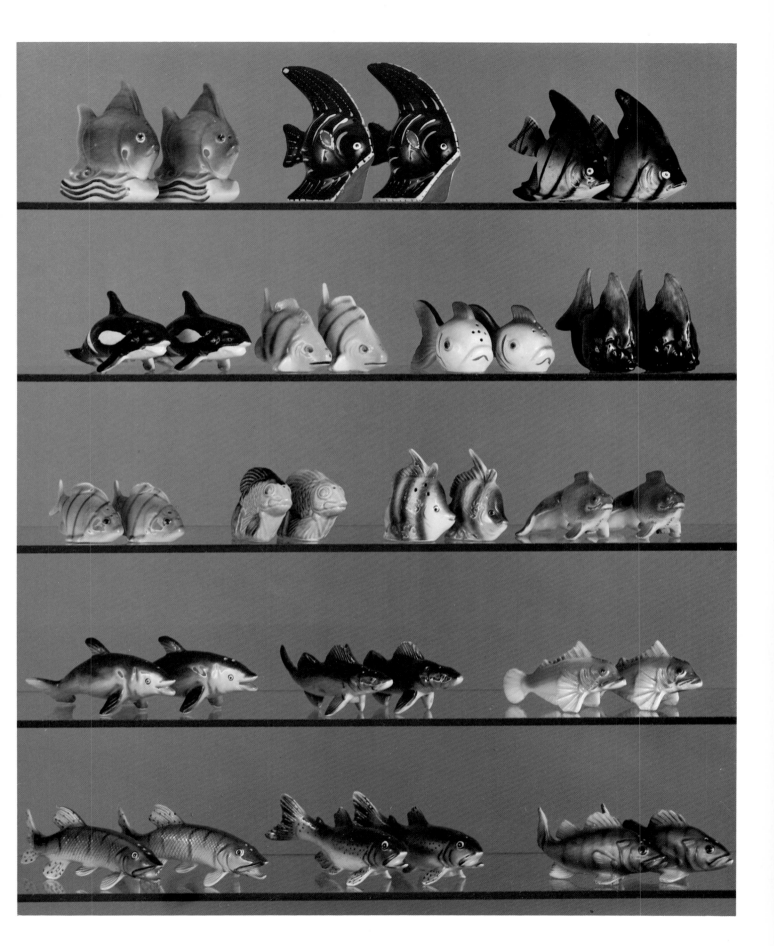

WOOD

Welcome to the wonderful and wacky world of wood! One must admit, however, that the sets on this page are exceptional for wooden shakers. The sets at the end of both Rows One and Two contain those never-to-sqeak squeakers! In the center of Row Two, the pepper shaker has a grinder for freshly ground pepper. The center set in Row One as well as all the sets in Row Four are rather unusual and are not as easily found as the rest. If you look closely at the soldiers (third set bottom row) you will see that they are marked "North" and "South." The first set in the same row fits together to look like one shaker.

All of the sets in Rows One and Two and the second set in Row Three as well as the soldiers are marked "Japan." The rest of the sets are unmarked. Although the wooden sets are harder to date than other shakers, I believe that those pictured date from the late 1940's to the last few years.

The second page in this section has a rather amusing story connected with it. Once our wonderful photographer Tom had checked the negative for this page and found that it was blurred, we had to photograph this page again. (We were probably laughing so hard over this particular selection of shakers that we bumped the camera!) My assistant, Carol – always the epitome of efficiency – had already re-packed the shakers for the return trip home, but we did our best to find the sets that had been photographed for this page. In spite of our efforts, we could locate only nine of the original seventeen sets but, take my word for it, you didn't miss a thing. (If you care to, you can drop Tom a note thanking him for saving you from the original selection!)

In Row One, the first and last shakers are a set. The each rest in a holder. The tall penguin in Row One and the second set in Row Two are shakers made to fit together to look like one shaker. Sets one and four in Row Two have magnets to hold them together – now, isn't that special?

The last two sets on the page have a dual purpose: the shakers hang *on* the fence and one can store napkins *in* the fence! The bull heads in the holders are marked "Japan" and were distributed by Enesco. The last set is dated 1956 and titled "The Corral Pals."

The selection on the last page of this section is rather common. The set of barrels in Row One is marked "Japan"; the tops unscrew to fill the shakers. The third set in Row Two is almost certainly a 1940's set featuring soldiers. In Row Three, the television sets, complete with pictures, are quite nice.

Rows Four and Five feature the jigsaw sets. I think I can safely say that the sets featured here are of 1940's-1950's vintage.

A wonderful and interesting display using ALL wooden shakers was exhibited by Kay Ramsey at our 1988 convention.

PAGE 165:
Row 1: (1) $10.00-$12.00   (2) $12.00-$15.00   (3) $10.00-$12.00
Row 2: All Sets: $8.00-$10.00
Row 3: (1) $5.00-$7.00   (2) $8.00-$10.00   (3) $5.00-$7.00
Row 4: (1) $7.00-$9.00   (2) $12.00-$15.00   (3) $12.00-$15.00   (4) $10.00-$12.00

PAGE 166:
Row 1: (1) $8.00-10.00   (2) $7.00-$9.00   (3) $7.00-$9.00   (4) $8.00-$10.00
Row 2: (1) $7.00-$9.00   (2) $7.00-$9.00   (3) $12.00-$15.00   (4) $7.00-$9.00
Row 3: set $10.00-$12.00
Row 4: set $10.00-$12.00

PAGE 167:
All sets: $5.00-$7.00

165

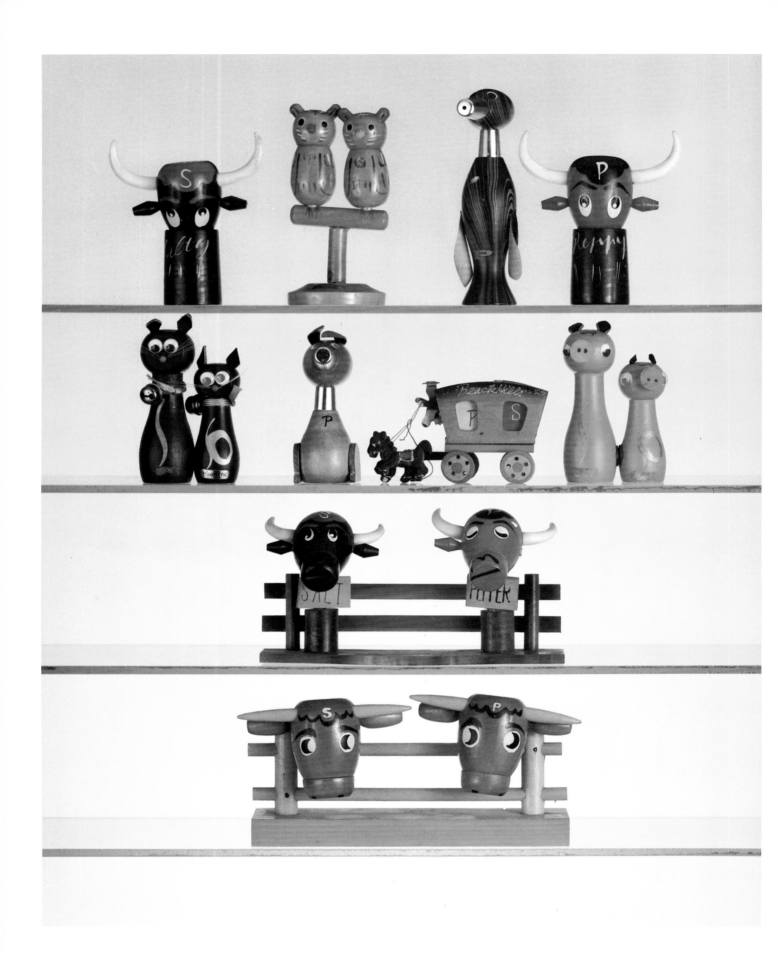

GO-WITHS: Animals and Things

This is another selection of fun sets, the type most collectors look for. The first set in Row One features a worm with a pear instead of the usual apple – humorous touch well appreciated by those of us who admire the diversity of these sets. The duck "carrier" set in the center of the row is rather unusual. The camel set was made in China and is made of porcelain.

In Row Two, the pig and his companion sausage form a rather bizarre set. I wonder if the sausage was once one of his friends!

The mouse and bowling pin and the donkey with the horseshoe in Row Three appear to be from the same series while the center set in the same row is a poor replica of the RCA Victor set.

In Row Four, the center set is a very desirable scarecrow with a cow; possibly from Poinsettia Studios, California. It would really be a super set to add to one's collection. As you may have suspected by now, go-withs are often difficult to match. The first set in Row Four is a good example of this. Since the coloring and glaze seem to match, it may be an authentic pair, but I have my doubts. In any event, this is how I received the set.

The center set in Row Five again demonstrates the delicious humor often found in these novelty shakers. On one shaker, the fish is safely inside a glass fishbowl while, on the other, the cat just sits staring, thinking naughty cat thoughts. This set is even nicer because someone actually cared enough to sign it. It was made by Menschik-Goldman, Inc. and dated 1960. Let's give this company (which was located in New York) a big hand for identifying this prize! We can also applaud the manufacturers of the last set pictured. This well-done set consists of a nicely painted skunk with a flower. It is signed by Poinsettia Studios, California, and is gold-trimmed, with a finish comparable to that of the Ceramic Arts Studio.

Although mostly unmarked, all of the sets in Row Two and Row Three, the pear and the worm in Row One and the last two sets in Row Five are believed to be American. The rest of the sets are Japanese. All of the shakers are ceramic except for the camel in Row One (which, as previously mentioned, was made in China.) The sets were manufactured for the most part in the 1950's and 1960's.

Row 1:	(1) $15.00-$18.00	(2) $22.00-$25.00	(3) $15.00-$18.00
Row 2:	(1) $12.00-$15.00	(2) $8.00-$10.00	(3) $8.00-$10.00
Row 3:	(1) $10.00-$12.00	(2) $12.00-$15.00	(3) $12.00-$15.00
Row 4:	(1) $12.00-$15.00	(2) $18.00-$22.00	(3) $15.00-$18.00
Row 5:	(1) $12.00-$15.00	(2) $28.00-$32.00	(3) $30.00-$35.00

GO-WITHS: Foods

This section will be without a doubt, the most popular one in the book. "Sticking my neck out" in my usual way, I will say that I believe the go-withs are the favorites of more than half of the novelty shaker collectors.

The name "Go-Withs" may need a word of explanation. Since these shakers do not match but are totally different from one another, the usual question which so many people ask is, "What does this go with?"...therefore the term "Go-Withs." Matching these delightful sets is a little like playing the old association game: I name an object and you tell me the first word that comes into your head. For instance, in the first row we have "pop and popcorn"; in Row Two "toast and toaster," "rolling pin and pie" and, of course, in Row Three, we find that all-time favorite..."coffee and doughnuts." Although collectors often ask which shakers go with each other, this section deals with those sets that specifically merit the title of "Go-Withs."

The nesters pictured here also fall into this category. The sundae in its cup, the banana split in its dish, the frying egg, pie a la mode, the pig nestled on the platter and the roasting turkey are all wonderful, fun "Go-Withs" sets.

The ice cream cones in Row One, however, and the unique stack of crackers in Row Four as well as all the sets in Row Five do not fall into the Go-Withs category. They are pictured in this section in order to keep all the novelty shakers representing food together. Of course, they do often "go with" many of us, as we go in to watch TV with our snacks!

The crackers were produced by "Medelman" in Italy. The sets in the last row were all made in Japan in the 1980's and so are relatively new. They are all, however, delightfully mouth-watering to look at.

Surprisingly, none of the other sets are marked with the exception of the egg in the frying pan which is marked "Bernard Studios Inc., Fullerton, California." I do believe that ALL of the unmarked sets were made here in the United States. We have so little information on the wonderful small potteries and ceramic houses that did these sets. If anyone has any information about any of these companies, please write to me and let me know. There MUST by someone out there who may have worked for one of these potteries at one time and it would be helpful to gather this information together. I would love to credit these wonderful sets to those who deserve our thanks.

In addition, I am always looking for old catalogs and salt-and-pepper club newsletters where they sold many of these sets we collect today. Take heed, folks! Start saving some of those gift catalogs you receive today in order to help the collectors of the future. Even sets which are new to us today will eventually become old and very collectible and in order to preserve the history of these new sets, it is our responsibility to save what information we can. Otherwise, the origin of these new sets will be as difficult to trace as the older sets we are now trying to document.

Row 1: (1) $22.00-$25.00	(2) $18.00-$22.00	(3) $8.00-$10.00	(4) $22.00-$25.00
Row 2: (1) $8.00-$10.00	(2) $10.00-$12.00	(3) $8.00-$10.00	(4) $12.00-$15.00
Row 3: (1) $8.00-$10.00	(2) $15.00-$18.00	(3) $12.00-$15.00	(4) $12.00-$15.00
Row 4: (1) $22.00-$25.00	(2) $18.00-$20.00	(3) $10.00-$12.00	
Row 5: (1) $8.00-$10.00	(2) $6.00-$8.00	(3) $8.00-$10.00	

GO-WITHS: Household Items and Tools

Many of us have been in touch with a lovely lady named Sue Campbell from Colorado who decorates doll houses with shakers! The last time I heard from her, I believe she had nine houses furnished. I hope to get out there to see them sometime: looking at the sets on this page, I can clearly imagine how someone could furnish a doll house with them.

The fireplace and the little bed in Row Two are nesters and are very popular sets. The chairs, however, are not "Go-Withs." The seats of these chairs, incidentally, have a scene of Niagara Falls on them! Although the photograph does not show the seat, they are made to snap into the wire frames of the chair and are marked "Japan." The table and chairs in the center of Row Two are stamped "Foreign." This means that, although they were made in Japan, they were exported to England or another foreign country, not to the United States. It does seem odd that items stamped "Foreign" and items stamped "Japan" are all from the same place, depending upon where the items are to be shipped – but that's international trade, I suppose.

The third set in both Row Three and Four was made in Japan. The sticker which is visible on the anvil is from Fern Imports, one of the many distributors for items made in Japan.

All of the sets are ceramic. And again, the remaining sets are unmarked and I believe, American-made. It is possible, and I believe probable, that may of them were made by Arcadia Ceramics, Arcadia, California. This is the same company that gave us most of the wonderful little miniature shakers that all collectors are shelling out their eye teeth for today! I have come across several sets in my collecting travels that have had Arcadia stickers on them. The finish of the ceramic as well as the manner in which the base is finished leads me to believe that many of these unmarked sets were made by Arcadia and the stickers have simply been removed along the way.

In addition, I also think that Parkcraft was responsible for some of the unmarked shaker sets as well as Arcadia, and since this is only an opinion, I would welcome any further information and/or discussion on the origin of these sets.

The sets pictured here account for some of the more popular "Go-Withs." The couch and chair at the end of Row Two are nicely done and not very easily found. In the center of Row Three is a chopping block and meat cleaver. The tool sets are popular as well and there are many varieties to be found.

Looking at the tire and pump reminds me of the wonderful birthday present my husband buys me every year....a membership in the American Automobile Association. It is a well-used gift! The lunch bucket and thermos in this section, incidentally, is included because they usually travel where the tools go!

Row 1:	(1) $12.00-$15.00	(2) $10.00-$12.00	(3) $8.00-$10.00
Row 2:	(1) $22.00-$25.00	(2) $28.00-$30.00	(3) $22.00-$25.00
Row 3:	(1) $18.00-$20.00	(2) $22.00-$25.00	(3) $12.00-$15.00
Row 4:	(1) $12.00-$15.00	(2) $22.00-$25.00	(3) $15.00-$18.00
Row 5:	(1) $22.00-$25.00	(2) $12.00-$15.00	(3) $10.00-$12.00

GO-WITHS: Music and Flowers

Ah how wonderful! The first signs of Spring, the soft sounds of music, the sweet smell of flowers and a few of those darn insects and other pests characteristic of the season!

The first two rows of shakers cover the music. The third set in Row One has both salt and pepper shakers and a napkin holder (the large piece in the center). This set was made in Taiwan and is made of porcelain. Unlike most shakers, the music books in the center of Row Two are easily dated, since 1955 is printed on the binding of the books. I'm sure that there are people who base their entire collection on sets in the form of musical instruments and related objects!

Some of the flowers I have seen in my travels (in shaker form, of course!) are so lovely and natural looking. The first set in Row Three is porcelain; the flowers are painted in very bright colors and there is a beautiful mixture in each pot. In addition, as you can see, the pots are different styles, adding to the interest. The second set in the row is American-made from the early 1940's. The last set in Row Three is porcelain, as is wonderful basket of flowers in the center of Row Four. Unless otherwise noted, the remaining sets are all ceramic.

Now...the bottom! Queasy collectors do not include these in their collections, I'll bet! I think the first pair is just charming...found them in a tomato last July. One must admit, they ARE cute. The lady bugs can be found in many colors and sizes, which can lead to an interesting collection within a collection. The set of butterflies, however, merits more serious attention. Since this delicate set traveled to Kentucky twice (there was no room for them in Book I), I must say I do not know how these beautiful shakers survived! The ironic part is that, as soon as I got back from photographing the shakers for this book, I again shipped them off to a friend in New Zealand. They arrived safely, and besides being a most interesting set of shakers, they may very well be the most-traveled butterflies around. And, as for the last set on this page, I will keep my comments to myself. After raising three sons, I found the real thing in too many places to mention.

All of the sets in Row Two and the worms in the last row are not marked but they do have the "American-made" look. Unless otherwise stated, the remaining sets were marked in Japan and all sets were manufactured mainly during the 1940-1950 era.

Row 1: (1) $6.00-$8.00   (2) $10.00-$12.00   (3) $12.00-$15.00 set
Row 2: (1) $10.00-$12.00   (2) $8.00-$10.00   (3) $12.00-$15.00
Row 3: All Sets: $6.00-$8.00
Row 4: (1) $12.00-$15.00   (2) $8.00-$10.00   (3) $10.00-$12.00
Row 5: (1) $12.00-$15.00   (2) $10.00-$12.00   (3) $15.00-$18.00   (4) $10.00-$12.00

GO-WITHS: People and Things

Many of the sets pictured here are nesters: all the sets in the first row, the angel in the center of Row Two, the monkeys at the end of Row Three, and the Mexican in the center of the last row.

The first set in Row One features a happy bride and groom on their way to Niagara Falls. The next set is interesting because the shakers are the smoke stacks on the ship and the entire set is nicely done, especially with the tiny sailor peering through his spyglass. The driving bear is a part of an amusing series of shakers made up of various animals in little cars.

In Row Two, the first set would really be fun to use. She is one shaker, her bust is the other one. If I had any prudish friends, I would invite them over for dinner and use these shakers! The next set, an adorable angel on a swan, is just delightful. It is carefully painted in pastels with a matte bisque-like finish and would certainly make a nice addition to any collection. The last set in this row is a favorite of many collectors. Could she be praying for a MAN? Well, if so, he is just under her bed!

All of the sets in Row Three are earlier ones, c. 1940's. There is a complete series of the "Monkey and Instrument" shakers. Both of the sets pictured here are porcelain, as are the first two sets in Row Five. The frog-and-drum shakers in Row Three are ceramic along with the rest of the sets not already mentioned.

In Row Four, we span the globe: Two Eskimo sets complete with igloos and in the center, a camel and Arab. The three sets in Row Five are from the 1940's and are distinguished by their older look. The little gnome under the mushroom, especially, is also nicely painted.

The first and last sets in Row Two and all the sets in Row Four are not marked but appear to be American-made. The rest of the sets are Japanese and range from the 1950's.

Row 1:	(1) $25.00-$28.00	(2) $10.00-$12.00	(3) $22.00-$25.00
Row 2:	(1) $25.00-$30.00	(2) $28.00-$32.00	(3) $18.00-$22.00
Row 3:	All Sets: $18.00-$20.00		
Row 4:	(1) $12.00-$15.00	(2) $18.00-$20.00	(3) $12.00-$15.00
Row 5:	(1) $10.00-$12.00	(2) $15.00-$18.00	(3) $10.00-$12.00

GO-WITHS: People and Things (continued)

There are indeed some wonderful sets on this page, I'm sure most of us can relate to the first set. This is the couple from the last book who wished they had danced all night instead! Remember? Their eyes are circled with dark shadows with a definite 3 a.m. look. This is a very popular and rather hard-to-find set. (There is a similar set in the turnabout section.) The second set is a pair of ship's captains who are now part of the fleet watching over Sylvia Tompkins' water-related collection!

The first set in Row Two, which I call "The Streetcleaner," is a part of a series which can be recognized by the very sparse painting on all of them. They are, I believe, American-made. The next set has always been a favorite of mine. Although I had this set long ago, I sold it. I have finally added it to my collection again, and this time I do plan to keep it! This brightly painted set has some wonderful features--not the least of which is the feeling I get that this particular milkman is about to run for his life. The next set is also a great addition to any collection-who can resist an organ grinder and his monkey?

In Row Three, the set of railroad conductors is handsomely painted and a rather rare set to find today. The fisherman have fish on their backs-a potentially smelly situation by the end of the day! Although the little boy and his camera are often mismatched, when they are correctly paired as they are here, they form a good set.

This is one of my favorite rows of shakers. The first set is a United Parcel Service driver on his way to MARS and the MOON here in Pittsburgh-Mars, Pennsylvania and Moon Township, Pennyslvania! Next you see one of my favorite mail carriers, "Lenny the Mailman," showing a new carrier the ropes. The last set in Row Four is such a long-time favorite of so many collectors that it is one of the shakers being reproduced today.

In the last row, the cooks are very nicely detailed and are a great set to own. The hunter and the rabbit are a very cute pair, but if the hunter was looking and aiming in the same direction, he'd be much better off! The last set in the row is a brewmaster, a nicely done but relatively common set.

The streetcleaner in Row Two and the hunter and rabbit in the last row are unmarked but assumed to be American. The remaining sets are Japanese. The milkman and cow set is porcelain, the rest ceramic.

Row 1:	(1) $22.00-$25.00	(2) $35.00-$45.00	
Row 2:	(1) $12.00-$15.00	(2) $30.00-$35.00	(3) $15.00-$18.00
Row 3:	(1) $15.00-$20.00	(2) $10.00-$12.00	(3) $22.00-$25.00
Row 4:	(1) $35.00-$40.00	(2) $15.00-$18.00	(3) $12.00-$15.00
Row 5:	(1) $15.00-$20.00	(2) $15.00-$18.00	(3) $12.00-$15.00

GO-WITHS: People and Things (continued)

The shakers in this section are included under the "Go-Withs" because they are paired with something other than another person. The set of gnomes in the center of Row One are not "Go-Withs"; they are included in this category, however, so that they are with the rest of the gnomes. The two sets of gnomes with animals which are on either side of Row One are from a 1979 line of shakers signed Unieboek. I do not know how many sets were in the series, but you can be sure there were more than just the two sets pictured. It would be interesting to have a completed series, especially since the shakers are so very nicely done.

In Row Two we have the Moonshine Boys! The first hillbilly has already had too much to drink...he can't even get up! The second one has a jug of "Snake Bite" in his arms and I can almost guarantee it's at least 90 proof. The little Mexican man, however, is not to be outdone. He has suspended two jugs from the ends of his mustache. This is an unusual set...in more ways than one.

Row Three presents a bull and matador which surprisingly still have all the red paint intact. In the center, two of my regular customers from my former bartending days return to haunt me. Embossed on the base of this set is a saying that has proven to be quite true. It reads: "There is one in every bar."

The last set in Row Three was made by Fitz and Floyd. This is a wonderfully amusing set to add to your collection. They are truly "jail birds!" You will find several other Fitz and Floyd sets in other sections of this book. They have issued several series since the late 1970's until the present.

All three sets in the last row are very popular. Thank heaven for lamp posts or neither of the gentlemen would be upright! The set in the center is one of my favorites. This one reads, "Goodbye Cruel World." Rather a drastic measure, wouldn't you say?

All of these sets were made in Japan. The center set in Row Three was made from red clay; the rest are ceramic. Shakers not dated above are from the 1950's.

Row 1:	All Sets: $18.00-$20.00		
Row 2:	(1) $10.00-$12.00	(2) $15.00-$18.00	(3) $22.00-$25.00
Row 3:	(1) $15.00-$18.00	(2) $22.00-$25.00	(3) $35.00-$40.00
Row 4:	(1) $12.00-$15.00	(2) $30.00-$35.00	(3) $22.00-$25.00

GO-WITHS: Sports

This is a very exciting section for the sports lover. The first row consists of three sets of dice and there are many other types of dice shakers to be found. The center set is very unusual. One shaker is a pair of dice and the other is a shaker in the shape of three playing cards. Each shaker rests on a "tee" type holder. These sets are very nicely done.

On Row Two, we cover boxing, fishing and weight lifting-all popular sports. The weight will set on the hand: it is better, however, to set it to one side as I have done because the shaker falls over from the slightest movement or touch when nested.

The first and third sets in Row Three represent one of the most popular sports of all time-FOOTBALL! In the middle of the row is a golf ball resting on a tee. Although I have always known that golf is another extremely popular sport, I never realized just how dedicated golfers were until I worked at a department store. I recall a man coming into the store to purchase ORANGE golf balls. Not being a golfer myself, I asked him, "Why the colored golf balls?" He just stared at me strangely as if I should have known the answer and then replied, "Orange balls are easier to find in the snow." This truly happened to me, but I never will know if he was really serious about golf in the SNOW!

The first set in Row Four has a special significance for me. Printed on the end of the mitt is "PITTSBURGH PIRATES." This is OUR team, and as a result this set of shakers will always remain in my collection. The last set in the row is an ordinary baseball and mitt. Last but not least, in the center of the last row is a set of binoculars and carrying case – something that automatically goes with most of the sports represented.

The first set in Row One is marked Taiwan, the second set was made in Japan and the remaining sets are unmarked. I believe that the unmarked sets are a part of the American-made shakers. You can be sure I will find out who made most of these sets eventually, but unfortunately it will be too late to print in this book!

Row 1: (1) $10.00-$12.00   (2) $15.00-$18.00   (3) $10.00-$12.00
Row 2: (2) $8.00-$10.00   (2) $12.00-$15.00   (3) $25.00-$30.00
Row 3: (3) $12.00-$15.00   (2) $18.00-$20.00   (3) $15.00-$18.00
Row 4: (4) $12.00-$15.00   (2) $12.00-$15.00   (3) $10.00-$12.00

183

GO-WITHS: Miscellaneous

This is a real miscellany of shakers, all "Go-Withs"; the cigar in the ashtray, the first set in Row Four, is the only nester set on this page. The thimble and thread in Row Two is marked C. C. Co. but, unfortunately, I could not find any information on it. The helmet and shield in the third row is marked M. V. Burig & Sons – no information on this one either. The mug and shaving brush in the center of the page is marked Trevewood. I discovered that this company was located in Roseville, Ohio and that is all I know about this one! All of the marks mentioned are impressed into the shaker and the same marks appear on several other sets throughout the book. None of the other sets in this section is marked; again, however, I believe that they were all made in the USA.

The watering can and flower in the center of Row Two is very nicely done and quite unusual. It is the only porcelain set on this page, the others all being ceramic.

I have been asked many times about the set with the screw and the 8-ball. This is without doubt an authentic set which was simply called the "Screwball" set in an old shaker club catalog. The skunk and cent is a real play on words too. Another set which is often confusing is the last set in Row Two combining both the gavel and Bible used by judges.

McArthur's hat and pipe is a very popular set (Row Five, center). I have talked with so many people who have just the hat and are searching for the pipe. All of these sets are fun to collect as well as being a challenge to match. The sets date from the 1950-1960 era.

Row 1:	(1) $18.00-$20.00	(2) $18.00-$20.00	(3) $15.00-$18.00
Row 2:	(2) $10.00-$12.00	(2) $18.00-$20.00	(3) $15.00-$18.00
Row 3:	(3) $22.00-$25.00	(2) $12.00-$15.00	(3) $15.00-$18.00
Row 4:	(4) $12.00-$15.00	(2) $12.00-$15.00	(3) $12.00-$15.00
Row 5:	(4) $15.00-$18.00	(2) $12.00-$15.00	(3) $12.00-$15.00

PEOPLE: Black Americana

The collecting of black items is very popular among both black and white collectors. This field is an extremely specialized area and the sets are collected for a wide variety of reasons. Since many sets depict a bigoted stereotype of the black race, many black people collect these items as a reminder of their history. The extremes of this era are far behind us (for which we may ALL be thankful) but I nevertheless offer my apologies to anyone who may be offended by the shakers in this section. My intention is soley to give the collectors of Black Americana some information to help them as I have done in other sections of this book.

Since I had decided to sell my collection of black items, including my shakers, prior to the publication of Book One, I must profusely thank collector friends whose generous sharing has made this section possible. Most of the sets are from the collection of Rich O'Donnell, a good friend from Bradenville, Pennsylvania. Not only did he lend me his sets, he also borrowed sets from his friends for me to use. Butch and Sandy Payne of Latrobe, Pennsylvania parted with their collection long enough to allow me to take it to Kentucky to be photographed, as did Lorraine Haywood of Westmont, Illinois. My deepest thanks to all of you.

Another note of gratitude to a Pittsburgh friend and my co-host of the 1987 convention, Betsy Zalewski, who lent me several sets for this section as well as other sets shown throughout the book.

Now, with all of that out of the way, let's go on to the sets pictured in the first row. The Mammy on the left and the Chef on the right form a rather tall set, which is basically unpainted except for the facial features and a little gold trim. The set is unmarked. The center set has a black chef's head and a white chef's head on a platter. I wonder whose meal they fouled up!!

Row Two features two wonderful sets. The boy and girl at each end of the shelf are simply great. I had always seem them as wall pockets and doubted those people who said that they also came in shaker form. Well...here they are! This set is unmarked, as are all the sets on this page, except for the set in the bottom row, which is marked "Japan." I do believe that many of these unmarked sets are American- made.

The china chef in the center of the page is truly a super find for collectors. He comes apart in three sections, the first two being the shakers and the bottom third a mustard pot.

The last row consists of the more common chef sets. I was told by a very nice gentleman at an Ohio flea market that many of the chef sets which are trimmed in gold, including the ones with the stoves in Book One, were made by the Stanford Pottery Company of Sebring, Ohio. The pottery closed after it was destroyed by fire in 1961. I do not positively know which sets they made but I do understand, however, that these sets were all trimmed in gold. This gives us at least one more puzzle piece to work with. Maybe someone out there has a Stanford Pottery catalog which would help to solve the ever more perplexing questions.

This entire page of shakers, which were made between the 1940's and the 1950's, is from the extensive Black Americana collection of Rich O'Donnell.

Row 1: (1) $75.00-$85.00 set	(2) $75.00-$85.00	(3) $75.00-$85.00 set
Row 2: (1) $200.00-$225.00 set	(2) $125.00-$140.00	(3) $200.00-$225.00 set
Row 3: (1) $75.00-$80.00	(2) $55.00-$65.00	(3) $85.00-$95.00

PEOPLE: Black Americana II

After having seven pages of black sets in Book One, I thought I must have cornered most of the field but, as you can see, I have included another seven pages of entirely different sets in this book. This page is one that drives collectors crazy to locate duplicate sets for their own collections.

Although the first set in Row One was on the cover of my first book, it was not on the inside, so I have included it again in order to describe the set in more detail to you. These comprise one of the nicest sets I have ever had. They are very delicately made of bisque and are beautifully detailed.

The whale in the center carries a little native boy who safely sits on a knob on the whale's head so that he cannot slide off into the very large mouth beneath him! The next set is also very nice, with two little native children with hand-painted shields.

In Row Two, the first set is crudely made and may have been a home-made set. The second set I feel should be on a tray of some kind, possibly with a mustard. I don't think it originally came with just the two shakers. The last set is two darling children, very nicely done.

There are six sets of vegetable boys to be found. Three are pictured here and the other three are picutre in Book One. All of them are very desirable sets and are much sought after.

The first set in Row Four is rather amusing-she is really giving that poor guy an ear beating! Now, the second set looks like it should have a big POT in the middle! The last set features a girl with a black face similar to the one with a brown face pictured in Book One. The bottom row are all Eastern blacks. The first set in this row is made of china and was made in Germany.

All the sets pictured date from the 1940's - 1950's. Sets one and two in Row Two, all the sets in row Four and the elephant with the boy in the center of Row Five are unmarked; the remaining sets were made in Japan. The shakers pictured on this page are from the O'Donnell collection.

Row 1: (1) $75.00-$85.00   (2) $100.00-$125.00   (3) $60.00-$70.00
Row 2: (1) $55.00-$65.00   (2) $75.00-$85.00   (3) $155.00-$165.00
Row 3: All Sets: $85.00-95.00
Row 4: (1) $40.00-$45.00   (2) $55.00-$65.00   (3) $35.00-$45.00
Row 5: (1) $85.00-$95.00   (2) $95.00-$100.00   (3) $40.00-$45.00

189

PEOPLE: Black Americana III

This page of shakers may also send collectors out on a frantic seek-and-search mission! The first set in Row One is the Valentine boy and girl. (Some of you remember the Valentine man and lady in Book One, done in the same style.) The second set, which is very unusual, is made of lightweight composition, nicely detailed. The last set has a dark brown glaze over red clay.

In Row Two, the first set is delightful (and thus very hard to find). The melons themselves are the shaker and the chef merely serves to hold them. The boy on the toilet is the same as the one pictured in Book One, except that this set is about an inch taller. The last set can be found in several poses and sizes; the boy is the salt and the melon the pepper.

In Row Three, the center set is titled "Chief Coffee Maker," and he carries two coffee pots. The man and the lady that flank each side of this shelf are from the Brayton Laguna Pottery, Laguna Beach, California. The plant opened in 1927 and was forced to close in 1963 due to the successfully competitive Japanese imports. There is a matching cookie jar of the lady, but I do not believe that one was made of the man. A note of interest to the avid Black Americana collector about this popular set: in 1951, the shakers were sold for $1.75 and the cookie jar for $6.25! Those were truly the days, my friends, (This information was supplied by Trish Claar, along with many other tidbits found throughout the book...thanks, Trish!)

The bottom row consists of Mammy-and-Chef sets, except for the set in the middle, which appears to be, for lack of better words to describe them, another homemade creation.

The Brayton Laguna set and all the sets in the last row are American-made during the 1940's and 1950's with the remaining sets having been made in Japan. Again, all the shakers are from the collection of Rich O'Donnell-that lucky man!!!

Row 1: (1) $140.00-$160.00   (2) $85.00-$90.00   (3) $75.00-$80.00
Row 2: (1) $125.00-$150.00   (2) $85.00-$95.00   (3) $150.00-$175.00
Row 3: (1) $125.00-$135.00 set (2) $185.00-$200.00 (3) $125.00-$135.00 set
Row 4: (1) $45.00-$50.00   (2) $65.00-$70.00   (3) $45.00-$55.00

PEOPLE: Black Americana IV

A selection to drool over, the shakers in Rows One and Two are from Lorraine Haywood's collection. The first set in Row One is quite amusing. While she looks as if she is wondering just how to pluck this chicken, he is busy preparing to cook it! This well-executed set has a fine glaze to add to its appeal. The next set, also nicely detailed, is an unusual variation of the Mammy-and-Chef theme in shakers.

Row Two has some wonderful very-hard-to-find sets. The boy and girl on either end are separate sets; each holds a slice of melon which is a shaker and they themselves constitute the second shaker. In the center is a super variation of the man-with-melon-slice motif. Great sets, Lorraine....thanks so much!

The next three rows of shakers which belong to Sandy and Butch Payne are also mouth-watering sets for the collector. The first set in Row Three was made in Germany and is beautifully detailed bisque. The third set in this row, a souvenir of New Orleans, is a plastic one-piece set. The other two sets are Mammy-and-Chef variations which are unusual in comparison with others in this size.

In Row Four, the first set similar to the set on the second page of this section but closer examination reveals a bit of difference. The chefs with tall hats and wide grin, however, would brighten up any collection; the last set in this row in particular is worthy of note because it is very uncommon.

The policeman are souvenir shakers from Nassau and are marked as such on the bottoms. Another extremely unusual set is the black Granny in the rocker-the only one of this type I have ever seen. It is really a super set!

The majority of the shakers on this page were made in Japan and all of them are from the 1940-1950 era.

Note: Some of the shaker sets were switched around during the photography session. As a result, I have inadvertently credited the large chefs on the top shelf on the right to Lorraine Haywood's collection whereas, they are really part of the Payne collection. The black Granny, however, belongs to Lorraine and not the Paynes as stated before. Now we are all confused!

Row 1: (1) $175.00-$185.00   (2) $95.00-$100.00
Row 2: (1) $100.00-$125.00   (2) $115.00-$125.00   (3) $100.00-$125.00
Row 3: (1) $125.00-$135.00   (2) $35.00-$40.00   (3) $45.00-$50.00   (4) $30.00-$35.00
Row 4: (1) $40.00-$45.00   (2) $45.00-$50.00   (3) $45.00-$50.00
Row 5: (1) $25.00-$30.00   (2) $70.00-$80.00   (3) $35.00-$40.00

193

PEOPLE: Black Americana V

This page consists of variations of Mammy-and-Chef sets and three sets of just plain Mammies. The large set in the middle of Row One is possibly a copy of the Pearl China set because it appears to be too poorly painted to be genuine Pearl. The Mammies to the right of this set are also crudely done but the first set in this row is just adorable and rather unusual.

All three sets in the middle row appear to have been poorly made and carelessly painted, they were most likely molded from the original sets. All these sets, however, are collectible so don't pass them up!

The shakers in the last row are all nice. The first set can be found in several different sizes and if one is extremely lucky, one may also find the cookie jar to match. The Mammy sets, dating from the late 1930's, have different size holes in each shaker. Although I believe that the last set in this row may be a copy of the plastic F & F shakers, these shakers are nicely finished, unlike other copies.

Only the first two sets in Row Three are marked "Japan"; the others are all unmarked. All sets are through the courtesy of the O'Donnell collection.

Row 1:	(1) $85.00-$95.00	(2) $85.00-$95.00	(3) $45.00-$55.00
Row 2:	(1) $65.00-$70.00	(2) $40.00-$45.00	(3) $65.00-$70.00
Row 3:	(1) $85.00-$95.00	(2) $125.00-$135.00	(3) $55.00-$65.00

PEOPLE: Black Americana VI

It was a pleasure putting together such a super page of the "three-inch-and-under" shakers. Since there are many of the same molds painted differently, I will only describe the more unusual ones. Other paint variations of the same sets are included in Book One-if these sets differ in any way, the collector wants them all!

The little chef children, the first set in Row One, are beautifully hand-painted; each one holds a tray and they are "making eyes" at each other in a delightfully amusing way. The second set is fairly new and was made in Taiwan. These shakers come in a large set as well as this small set. The collector can also find a matching toothpick holder, cookie jar and bell. These pieces are all well-made bisque and they will all become old before we know it-so again don't pass them up because they are newer items. The last set on this shelf is a "kissing couple" which, although they are painted white, do have definite black features. This set also comes in blue.

The set in the center of Row Two is unusual because it is made of metal; it is a popular set and thus hard to find. In contrast, the "Rastus and Liza" set in the middle of Row Four is made of wood and is therefore plentiful and relatively easy to find.

In the bottom row, all the sets are from the same mold. The last set is marked Elbee Art, Cleveland, Ohio. This company manufactured several black sets, includind the minstrel man and his gloves pictured on page 127 in Book One. Elbee also advertised a 4½" Mammy-and-Chef set in a 1951 gift catalog. You may notice that several other sets throughout this book were also made by Elbee.

Unless otherwise stated these sets were made in Japan during the 1940's and the 1950's and they all belong to Rich O'Donnell.

Row 1: (1) $55.00-$65.00   (2) $20.00-$25.00   (3) $30.00-$35.00
Row 2: (1) $35.00-$45.00   (2) $35.00-$45.00   (3) $35.00-$40.00
Row 3: (1) $35.00-$45.00   (2) $35.00-$40.00   (3) $35.00-$40.00   (4) $45.00-$55.00
Row 4: (1) $30.00-$35.00   (2) $20.00-$25.00   (3) $30.00-$35.00
Row 5: All Sets: $30.00-$35.00

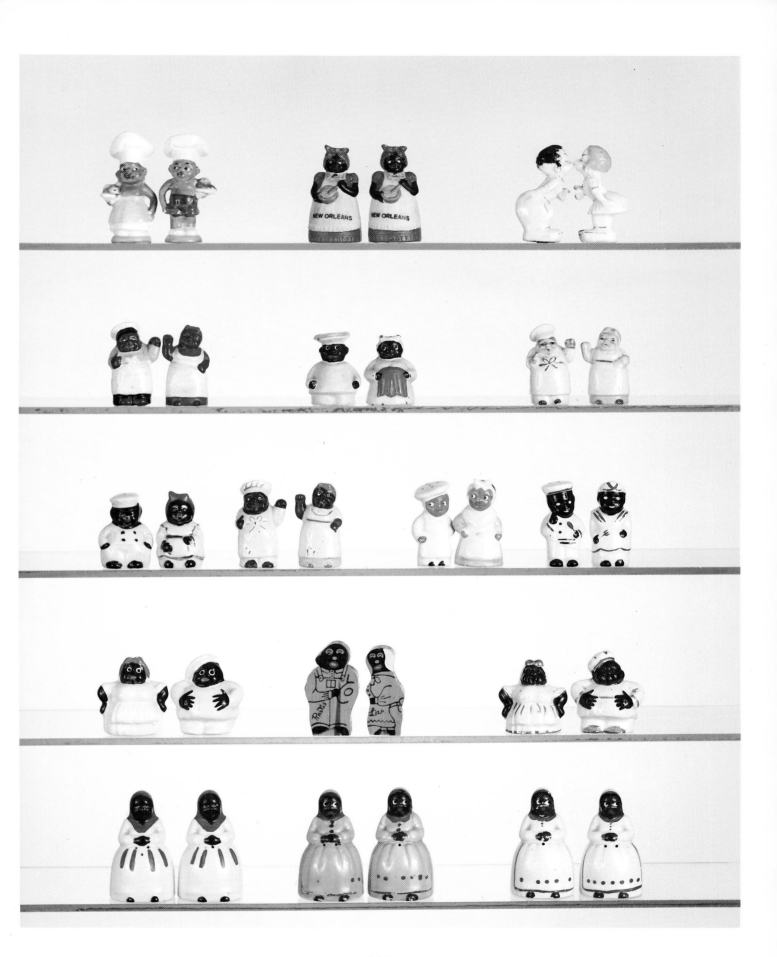

PEOPLE: Black Americana VII

Row One offers a small sampling of wooden shakers. The set in the center is quite different; there is a hole where the elephant's tail should be that is meant to hold toothpicks, as well as tiny holes all around the two "natives" which are used to hold hor d' oeuvres. Although wooden shakers are often considered to be too ordinary for most collections, these sets are rather nice and the last set, in fact, is rather unique.

The large shakers at each end of Row Two are of natives with decidedly exaggerated features. The center set, however, is very nice; the shakers are natives, the mustard pot is shaped like a native hut, and the entire ensemble rests on a tray.

The nicely-decorated sets in Row Three are also unusual. The first native has a drum and appears to be about to dance. The second set is comprised of two young boys doing what young boys seem to do so well-just hanging around! Although the last set may not be correctly paired, this is how I received them. Correctly matched or not, however, this set is very well done.

The spice rack on the bottom shelf has shakers which are shaped like books and the spine of each book is painted to look like a black chef. This type of set comes in several sizes with a varied number of containers.

The last set in Row One and all the sets in Row Three are from the collection of Betty Zalewski and the remaining sets belong to Rich O'Donnell. Thanks folks! All the sets, which date from the 1940's and 1950's were made in Japan.

Row 1: (1) $18.00-$20.00	(2) $25.00-$30.00	(3) $30.00-$35.00
Row 2: (1) $85.00-$95.00	(2) $95.00-$100.00	(3) $85.00-$95.00 set
Row 3: (1) $65.00-$75.00	(2) $55.00-$65.00	(3) $85.00-$95.00*
Row 4: Set: $85.00-$95.00		

*Note: Row three, set three is not a match. The correct set is the Native on a drum. Price for corrected set is $85.00-95.00.

PEOPLE: Children

This is always one of my favorite pages: children sets are so charming. The first set is the oldest one on this page, dating from the late 1930's or so, and exhibiting a definite "Betty Boop" look. These are made of china. The next two sets, which are bisque, are just darling. The second set in Row One is another Holt-Howard creation. The last set in this row are Kewpie-types and as such are very collectible. Those sets signed "Rose O'Neill" are of course the most sought after and the most valuable. This set, however, is not signed and is a Japanese copy.

The center set in Row Two is also a copy – this time of the Hummel Umbrella Children. (As I stated elsewhere in this book, Sylvia Tomkins of Lancaster seeks shakers that are even remotely water-related and she was delighted to add this set to her already extensive collection.)

The sets on each end of the second shelf, the Eskimos, Pilgrims and the Dutch children that fill the third row all have an appeal guaranteed to catch the collector's eye. The third set in Row Three, incidentally, is dated 1949 on the bottom of the shaker.

In Row Four, the first and third sets are from a series. I don't know how many are in the complete set. Each pair, however, is a different color and each of the angels in the set hold something different. Dot Gammon from Memphis has more complete series than any other collector I know. Her husband has built her a house just for her shakers which is lovingly dubbed "Dot's Shaker Shack," where she has more than 15,000 sets beautifully displayed.

The center set in the last row is made of pottery and was made in the late 1970's. The boys with the flutes at the end of the page, the blue-and-white angels in Row Four and the eskimos dated 1949 are all unmarked as to country or origin. The remaining shakers were made in Japan in the 1940's, 1950's and through the 1960's.

Row 1: (1) $25.00-$30.00	(2) $15.00-$18.00	(3) $18.00-$20.00	(4) $30.00-$35.00
Row 2: (1) $15.00-$18.00	(2) $18.00-$20.00	(3) $15.00-$18.00	
Row 3: (1) $12.00-$15.00	(2) $10.00-$12.00	(3) $8.00-$10.00	(4) $7.00-$9.00
Row 4: (1) $10.00-$12.00	(2) $10.00-$12.00	(3) $10.00-$12.00	
Row 5: (1) $10.00-$12.00	(2) $8.00-$10.00	(3) $8.00-$10.00	

PEOPLE: Indians

For collectors who specialize in this area, there is an interestingly varied selection of Indians. Because of the colorful headdresses, costumes and tribal trappings, the Indian shakers are all very appealing.

The first set of the top shelf is a pair of Thunderbird totems which are made of wood. The second set appears to be also made of wood, but it is instead made of ceramic and is quite strange looking with a hand-carved appearance. The set of teepees at the end of the row were made of a composition material which resembles wood. Many items were made by Multi-Products in the 1940's and early 1950's and they all have the date impressed in them – a real boon to the collector.

The center set in Row Two is a mustard set; the teepee is the mustard and the Indians are the shakers. The next set is also a three-piece set, but the canoe in this instance serves only as a holder for the shakers. A really unusual set is in the center of the page – the bottom portion of the shaker is wood and the heads are ceramic.

The first and last sets in Row Four are the very popular type known as "kissing couples." (I know several collectors who specialize in this type of shaker.) The first set has the appearance of shakers made by the Goebel Company of Germany, but these are marked "Japan."

The center set in the last row is chalkware. The sets on each end are not marked; I believe, however, that they are American-made.

Unless otherwise mentioned, all the sets are ceramic and were made in Japan between 1940 and 1950.

Row 1: (1) $8.00-$10.00	(2) $10.00-$12.00	(3) $8.00-$10.00
Row 2: (1) $15.00-$18.00	(2) $25.00-$30.00	(3) $25.00-$30.00
Row 3: (1) $12.00-$15.00	(2) $10.00-$12.00	(3) $10.00-$12.00
Row 4: (1) $20.00-$25.00	(2) $12.00-$15.00	(3) $12.00-$15.00
Row 5: (1) $12.00-$15.00	(2) $10.00-$12.00	(3) $18.00-$20.00

PEOPLE: Santa Claus and Christmas

Ho! Ho! Ho!...Off we go and, of course, Santa always leads the way. The first and third sets of Santa in Row One are similar but they carry different items. One set is marked "Shafford, Japan," a name one often sees on shakers. The center set is really cute. Santa is held by a magnet on top of a stack of gifts. This charming shaker is a Holt-Howard creation. This company, located in Stamford, Connecticut, produced some of their shakers but the majority were imported by them. Their peak years were during the 1950's and 1960's. Trish Claar, who has supplied this information, is one of the growing number of collectors who specializes in collecting Holt-Howard sets.

In Row Two, the wonderful nester in the center, also made by Shafford has long since retired to a collection in sunny California! The Santas in the chimneys are also nice variations.

The remaining sets on this page are rather more traditional Santas with the exception of the set on either end of Row Five. I've always wondered what they did out West with no snow...I'll bet Santa delivers gifts on horseback! In any event, these shakers feature Santa and his Missus all bedecked in western garb ready to deliver a pony or two. I must point out another oddity on the shelf above; where Mrs. Claus is wearing a green dress instead of her usual red one. This is a larger set than usual, but very nicely done.

The majority of sets are Japanese. The first set in Row Four was made in Taiwan and is relatively new. The remaining sets date from the 1940's to the 1960's.

Row 1:	(1) $12.00-$15.00	(2) $18.00-$20.00	(3) $10.00-$12.00
Row 2:	(1) $12.00-$15.00	(2) $18.00-$20.00	(3) $8.00-$10.00
Row 3:	(1) $12.00-$15.00	(2) $10.00-$12.00	(3) $6.00-$8.00	(4) $10.00-$12.00
Row 4:	(1) $10.00-$12.00	(2) $12.00-$15.00	(3) $12.00-$15.00
Row 5:	(1) $22.00-$25.00	(2) $10.00-$12.00	(3) $18.00-$20.00

205

205

PEOPLE: Santa and Christmas: (continued)

All of the sets on this page can be included in a Christmas collection and they certainly help to make a great Christmas display. The first set on the page, the wonderful little rocking horses, are beautifully decorated. They are labeled "Lefton," another name often found on shakers and one that is very collectible. The Lefton Company, in business since 1940, is a distributor of both imported and domestic items. The Rudolph set in Row Two is also Lefton. Hats off to them for being one of the companies who mark their wares!

Considering all the space travel these days, Santa has been asked for a lot of space toys, so he has had to do some importing. His two elves are ready to leave to pick up an order from the moon – as you can see from the last set in the top row!

Moving down to Row Two, the last two sets are wonderfully imaginative snowmen. There are just not enough snowmen around to satisfy those of us who collect, so these are really special. In the center row are the Christmas children or angels (as they all are at Christmas time!) The last set in this row were made by Holt-Howard.

Row Four features our only Christmas mouse set this time around. Although Book One pictured a set of elf boots, the set here is a bit smaller. Last but not least, the chipmunks are a "use at your own risk" set with rhinestone eyes that could add an unexpected bit of sparkle to your diet!!

The center set in Row Five is rather nice. It is metal and the tray has a scene of Santa at the North Pole. The two silver-coated reindeer are the shakers which rest on the tray. The two other sets in this row are simple but effective shakers for the holiday table.

Since different Christmas shakers are introduced every year, it is wise for the collector to purchase them as they become available. Once these sets are gone, they are gone for good so get them while you may!

With the exception of the Christmas mice, all the sets were made in Japan and date between 1940 and 1960.

Row 1:	(1) $12.00-$15.00	(2) $8.00-$10.00	(3) $18.00-$20.00
Row 2:	(1) $12.00-$15.00	(2) $10.00-$12.00	(3) $10.00-$12.00
Row 3:	(1) $8.00-$10.00	(2) $10.00-$12.00	(3) $12.00-$15.00
Row 4:	(1) $8.00-$10.00	(2) $8.00-$10.00	(3) $10.00-$12.00
Row 5:	(1) $6.00-$8.00	(2) $12.00-$15.00	(3) $5.00-$7.00

207

PEOPLE: Turnabouts

This section featuring double-faced shakers commonly known as "Turnabouts" is one of my favorites. The "before" side generally depicts a bride and groom for (or some variation thereof) while the reverse reveals the situation a few months (or years) later. These sets can be either quite humorous or depressing, depending upon one's point of view, but they are all unique. As you can see, there are many variations but all the sets are in demand. Several sets, however, are quite difficult to find. The second set in the first row is one of the most sought after-and one to which I can definitely relate. I wonder if this set was designed by new parents!

In the second row of Turnabouts, the last set is probably one of the most difficult sets to find in the entire world of shaker collecting. Unfortunately, I do not own this one: it belongs to Rich O'Donnell who was kind enough to lend it to me along with the rest of his Black Americana shaker collection. Rich, of course, held the deed to my house until I returned them all!

The first set on the page is rather common but interesting because it is comprised of a man and woman instead of the usual bride and groom. The shakers, however, are still "happy" before and "mad" afterwards, so nothing is really different except the attire.

Several sets look very much alike. The fourth set in Row One and the first set in Row Two, for example, are basically the same but, if you place them side by side, you will see that one set is a bit larger and is painted differently. Keep differences in mind when buying sets to add to your collections and know exactly what you have or you may miss out on sets by thinking you already have it.

I have had children and clown sets in the past and I am sure that there are many other variations to be found. Even if you found all the sets available, however, you would fill no more than a medium size cabinet. If space is a problem, therefore, Turnabouts might be a good area of specialization for you.

All sets are hand-painted ceramic and were made in Japan. Although it is possible that shakers of this type were made later, those pictured here date from the late 1940's through the early 1960's.

Row 1:(1) $12.00-$15.00	(2) $25.00-$30.00	(3) $23.00-$25.00	(4) $20.00-$25.00
Row 2:(1) $20.00-$25.00	(2) $15.00-$18.00	(3) $20.00-$25.00	(4) $175.00-$195.00

209

PEOPLE: Miscellaneous

The variety of shakers to be found never ceases to delight me! The next two pages feature people from every conceivable world, including the world of fantasy.

In Row One, the first set is nicely detailed with life-like features; the added touch of realism is furnished by the three-dimensional form of the woman's glasses and the man's pipe, both of which extend out from the body of the shaker. This set is also a bit taller than usual, as are the other two sets in this row. The Oriental couple has a brightly painted finish which almost possess the quality of pieces done by the Ceramic Arts Studio.

In Row Two, the kitchen witch is dated 1979 and was made in Taiwan. The kissing couple in the center of the row is one of a series which was called "Sweethearts of all Nations," produced by the National Potteries Companies (NAPCO) and sold in 1965. The set pictured is of a Swiss couple but many nations were represented in the series. This is another company that should be applauded for signing and dating most of their shakers. Their NAPCO trademark is often found on a paper sticker as well as on the items themselves. Although the bulk of their products was imported, they did manufacture some items, and in fact, they are still in operation today as distributors. To finish off this row is a well-finished and detailed Mexican couple who appear to be ready to dance off the page.

Although most of the shakers on this page are ceramic, the last set of Orientals in Row Three are china. Looks like the scarecrows in the next row got hanged for smooching!! Both of these scarecrow sets are great, especially the second set which hangs on a wire rack.

The center set in Row Five is very strange. This couple has very bizarre long pointed noses but nevertheless, the high-gloss paint which was used to decorate them makes this set highly desirable. The first set in Row Four and the end sets in this row are also avidly sought by collectors. Known as "Bench People," this type of shaker furnishes yet another area of specialization.

On the next page you will find the first three sets are American-made, company unknown. Row Two features two more Bench People sets.

The center row has three super sets. The wrestlers shown here also appeared in Book One, but I have since learned that they should fit into this body slam position, which I thought would interest some of you. The joggers are from the 1970's and are from a series of sports shakers. The little boys playing baseball are one of my favorite sets – they are so beautifully painted.

The hillbilly people make up Row Four and the last row of pixies is a subject very popular with collectors.

People sets are fun to collect and, as I am sure you noticed throughout this section, there are many opportunities to form specialty collections within this area.

Unless otherwise mentioned, all sets were made in Japan during the 1940 to 1960 era.

PAGE 211:
Row 1 (1) $12.00-$15.00	(2) $12.00-$15.00	(3) $8.00-$10.00
Row 2: (1) $12.00-$15.00	(2) $22.00-$25.00	(3) $12.00-$15.00
Row 3: (1) $8.00-$10.00	(2) $8.00-$10.00	(3) $7.00-$9.00
Row 4: (1) $12.00-$15.00	(2) $12.00-$15.00	
Row 5: (1) $10.00-$12.00	(2) $10.00-$12.00	(3) $10.00-$12.00

PAGE 212:
Row 1: (1) $8.00-$10.00	(2) $15.00-$18.00	(3) $8.00-$10.00
Row 2: (1) $8.00-$10.00	(2) $12.00-$15.00	
Row 3: (1) $25.00-$30.00	(2) $20.00-$25.00	(3) $20.00-$25.00
Row 4: (1) $8.00-$10.00	(2) $7.00-$9.00	(3) $10.00-$12.00
Row 5: (1) $6.00-$8.00	(2) $8.00-$10.00	(3) $12.00-$15.00

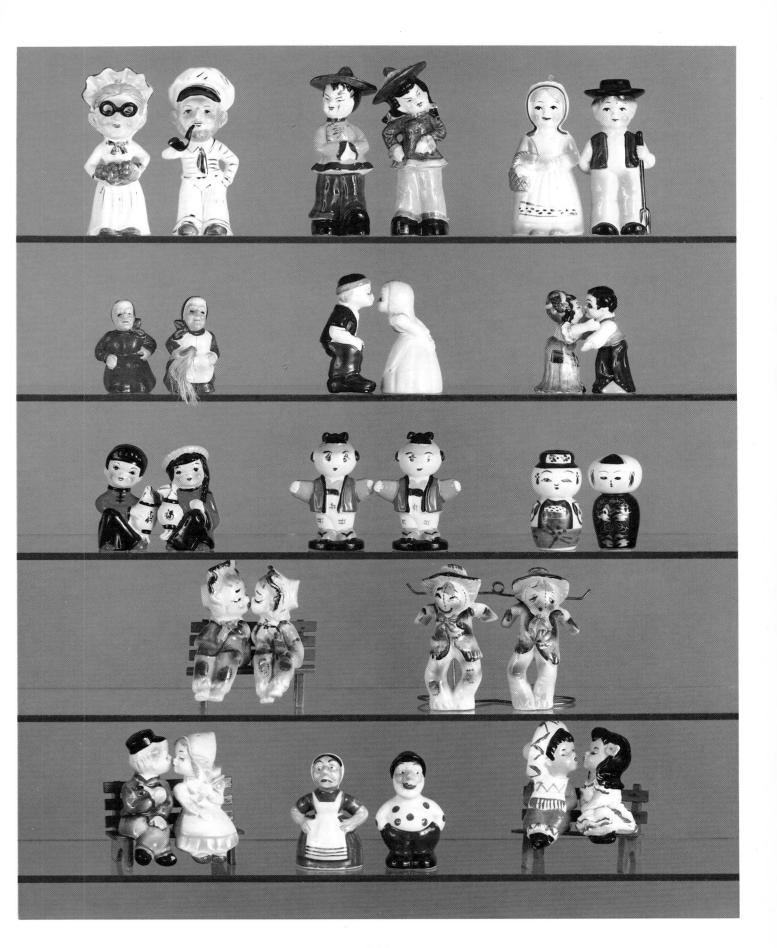

REACH OUT TO COLLECTORS

"Reach out" my friends, to other states
and lands across the way.
Seek out collectors near and far
and make new friends today.
Send a letter, make a call
to buy or sell or trade;
A shaker here----a shaker there---
that's how collections are made.
"Reach out"----no matter where you are
'cause somewhere 'round a bend
There's someone waiting just for you
so he can call you "Friend."

Melva R. Davern

**SECOND ANNUAL SALT AND PEPPER
CLUB CONVENTION SHAKERS--1987**

Books on Antiques and Collectibles

Most of the following books are available from your local book seller or antique dealer, or on loan from your public library. If you are unable to locate certain titles in your area you may order by mail from COLLECTOR BOOKS, P.O. Box 3009, Paducah, KY 42002-3009. This is only a partial listing of the books on antiques that are available from Collector Books. All books are well illustrated and contain current values. Add $2.00 for postage for the first book ordered and $.30 for each additional book. Include item number, title and price when ordering. Allow 14 to 21 days for delivery.

BOOKS ON GLASS AND POTTERY

1810	American Art Glass, Shuman	$29.95
2016	Bedroom & Bathroom Glassware of the Depression Years	$19.95
1312	Blue & White Stoneware, McNerney	$9.95
1959	Blue Willow, 2nd Ed., Gaston	$14.95
2270	Collectible Glassware from the 40's, 50's, & 60's, Florence	$19.95
3311	Collecting Yellow Ware - Id. & Value Gd., McAllister	$16.95
2352	Collector's Ency. of Akro Agate Glassware, Florence	$14.95
1373	Collector's Ency. of American Dinnerware, Cunningham	$24.95
2272	Collector's Ency. of California Pottery, Chipman	$24.95
3312	Collector's Ency. of Children's Dishes, Whitmyer	$19.95
2133	Collector's Ency. of Cookie Jars, Roerig	$24.95
2273	Collector's Ency. of Depression Glass, 10th Ed., Florence	$19.95
2209	Collector's Ency. of Fiesta, 7th Ed., Huxford	$19.95
1439	Collector's Ency. of Flow Blue China, Gaston	$19.95
1915	Collector's Ency. of Hall China, 2nd Ed., Whitmyer	$19.95
2334	Collector's Ency. of Majolica Pottery, Katz-Marks	$19.95
1358	Collector's Ency. of McCoy Pottery, Huxford	$19.95
3313	Collector's Ency. of Niloak, Gifford	$19.95
1039	Collector's Ency. of Nippon Porcelain I, Van Patten	$19.95
2089	Collector's Ency. of Nippon Porcelain II, Van Patten	$24.95
1665	Collector's Ency. of Nippon Porcelain III, Van Patten	$24.95
1034	Collector's Ency. of Roseville Pottery, Huxford	$19.95
1035	Collector's Ency. of Roseville Pottery, 2nd Ed., Huxford	$19.95
3314	Collector's Ency. of Van Briggle Art Pottery, Sasicki	$24.95
2339	Collector's Guide to Shawnee Pottery, Vanderbilt	$19.95
1425	Cookie Jars, Westfall	$9.95
2275	Czechoslovakian Glass & Collectibles, Barta	$16.95
3315	Elegant Glassware of the Depression Era, 5th Ed., Florence	$19.95
3318	Glass Animals of the Depression Era, Garmon & Spencer	$19.95
2024	Kitchen Glassware of the Depression Years, 4th Ed., Florence	$19.95
2379	Lehner's Ency. of U.S. Marks on Pottery, Porcelain & Clay	$24.95
2394	Oil Lamps II, Thuro	$24.95
3322	Pocket Guide to Depression Glass, 8th Ed., Florence	$9.95
2345	Portland Glass, Ladd	$24.95
1670	Red Wing Collectibles, DePasquale	$9.95
1440	Red Wing Stoneware, DePasquale	$9.95
1958	So. Potteries Blue Ridge Dinnerware, 3rd Ed., Newbound	$14.95
2221	Standard Carnival Glass, 3rd Ed., Edwards	$24.95
1848	Very Rare Glassware of the Depression Years, Florence	$24.95
2140	Very Rare Glassware of the Depression Years, Second Series	$24.95
3326	Very Rare Glassware of the Depression Era, Third Series	$24.95
3327	Watt Pottery - Identification & Value Guide, Morris	$19.95
2224	World of Salt Shakers, 2nd Ed., Lechner	$24.95

BOOKS ON DOLLS & TOYS

2079	Barbie Fashion, Vol. 1, 1959-1967, Eames	$24.95
3310	Black Dolls - 1820-1990 - Id. & Value Guide, Perkins	$17.95
1514	Character Toys & Collectibles 1st Series, Longest	$19.95
1750	Character Toys & Collectibles, 2nd Series, Longest	$19.95
1529	Collector's Ency. of Barbie Dolls, DeWein	$19.95
2338	Collector's Ency. of Disneyana, Longest & Stern	$24.95
2342	Madame Alexander Price Guide #17, Smith	$9.95
1540	Modern Toys, 1930-1980, Baker	$19.95
2343	Patricia Smith's Doll Values Antique to Modern, 8th ed	$12.95
1886	Stern's Guide to Disney	$14.95

2139	Stern's Guide to Disney, 2nd Series	$14.95
1513	Teddy Bears & Steiff Animals, Mandel	$9.95
1817	Teddy Bears & Steiff Animals, 2nd, Mandel	$19.95
2084	Teddy Bears, Annalees & Steiff Animals, 3rd, Mandel	$19.95
2028	Toys, Antique & Collectible, Longest	$14.95
1808	Wonder of Barbie, Manos	$9.95
1430	World of Barbie Dolls, Manos	$9.95

OTHER COLLECTIBLES

1457	American Oak Furniture, McNerney	$9.95
2269	Antique Brass & Copper, Gaston	$16.95
2333	Antique & Collectible Marbles, Grist, 3rd Ed.	$9.95
1712	Antique & Collectible Thimbles, Mathis	$19.95
1748	Antique Purses, Holiner	$19.95
1868	Antique Tools, Our American Heritage, McNerney	$9.95
1426	Arrowheads & Projectile Points, Hothem	$7.95
1278	Art Nouveau & Art Deco Jewelry, Baker	$9.95
1714	Black Collectibles, Gibbs	$19.95
1128	Bottle Pricing Guide, 3rd Ed., Cleveland	$7.95
1751	Christmas Collectibles, Whitmyer	$19.95
1752	Christmas Ornaments, Johnston	$19.95
2132	Collector's Ency. of American Furniture, Vol. I, Swedberg	$24.95
2271	Collector's Ency. of American Furniture, Vol. II, Swedberg	$24.95
2338	Collector's Ency. of Disneyana, Longest & Stern	$24.95
2018	Collector's Ency. of Graniteware, Greguire	$24.95
2083	Collector's Ency. of Russel Wright Designs, Kerr	$19.95
2337	Collector's Guide to Decoys, Book II, Huxford	$16.95
2340	Collector's Guide to Easter Collectibles, Burnett	$16.95
1441	Collector's Guide to Post Cards, Wood	$9.95
2276	Decoys, Kangas	$24.95
1629	Doorstops, Id. & Values, Betoria	$9.95
1716	Fifty Years of Fashion Jewelry, Baker	$19.95
3316	Flea Market Trader, 8th Ed., Huxford	$9.95
3317	Florence's Standard Baseball Card Price Gd., 5th Ed.	$9.95
1755	Furniture of the Depression Era, Swedberg	$19.95
2278	Grist's Machine Made & Contemporary Marbles	$9.95
1424	Hatpins & Hatpin Holders, Baker	$9.95
3319	Huxford's Collectible Advertising - Id. & Value Gd.	$17.95
1181	100 Years of Collectible Jewelry, Baker	$9.95
2023	Keen Kutter Collectibles, 2nd Ed., Heuring	$14.95
2216	Kitchen Antiques - 1790–1940, McNerney	$14.95
3320	Modern Guns - Id. & Val. Gd., 9th Ed., Quertermous	$12.95
1965	Pine Furniture, Our Am. Heritage, McNerney	$14.95
3321	Ornamental & Figural Nutcrackers, Rittenhouse	$16.95
2026	Railroad Collectibles, 4th Ed., Baker	$14.95
1632	Salt & Pepper Shakers, Guarnaccia	$9.95
1888	Salt & Pepper Shakers II, Guarnaccia	$14.95
2220	Salt & Pepper Shakers III, Guarnaccia	$14.95
3323	Schroeder's Antique Price Guide, 11th Ed.	$12.95
3324	Schroeder's Antique & Coll. 1993 Engag. Calendar	$9.95
2346	Sheet Music Ref. & Price Guide, Patik & Guiheen	$18.95
2096	Silverplated Flatware, 4th Ed., Hagan	$14.95
3325	Standard Knife Collector's Guide, Stewart	$12.95
2348	20th Century Fashionable Plastic Jewelry, Baker	$19.95
2349	Value Guide to Baseball Collectibles, Raycraft	$16.95

Schroeder's ANTIQUES Price Guide

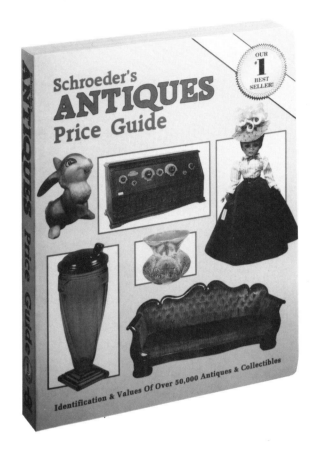

Schroeder's Antiques Price Guide is the #1 best-selling antiques & collectibles value guide on the market today, and here's why . . . More than 300 authors, well-known dealers, and top-notch collectors work together with our editors to bring you accurate information regarding pricing and identification. More than 45,000 items in almost 500 categories are listed along with hundreds of sharp original photos that illustrate not only the rare and unusual, but the common, popular collectibles as well. Each large close-up shot shows important details clearly. Every subject is represented with histories and background information, a feature not found in any of our competitors' publications. Our editors keep abreast of newly-developing trends, often adding several new categories a year as the need arises. If it merits the interest of today's collector, you'll find it in *Schroeder's*. And you can feel confident that the information we publish is up to date and accurate. Our advisors thoroughly check each category to spot inconsistencies, listings that may not be entirely reflective of market dealings, and lines too vague to be of merit. Only the best of the lot remains for publication. Without doubt, you'll find *Schroeder's Antiques Price Guide* the only one to buy for reliable information and values.

8½ x 11", 608 Pages   **$12.95**

COLLECTOR BOOKS

A Division of Schroeder Publishing Co., Inc.